Nudging

The Economy | Key Ideas

These short primers introduce students to the core concepts, theories and models, both new and established, heterodox and mainstream, contested and accepted, used by economists and political economists to understand and explain the workings of the economy.

Austerity
John Fender

Behavioural Economics
Graham Mallard

Bounded Rationality
Graham Mallard

Cultural Economics
Christiane Hellmanzik

Degrowth
Giorgos Kallis

Economic Anthropology
James G. Carrier

Financial Inclusion
Samuel Kirwan

The Gig Economy
Alex De Ruyter and Martyn Brown

Industrial Policy
Steve Coulter

The Informal Economy
Colin C. Williams

The Living Wage
Donald Hirsch and Laura Valadez-Martinez

Marginalism
Bert Mosselmans

Nudging
Mark Whitehead and Rhys Jones

Productivity
Michael Haynes

The Resource Curse
S. Mansoob Murshed

Nudging

Mark Whitehead and Rhys Jones

In loving memory of Dr Rachel Howell, friend, colleague, inspiration

First published in 2024 by Agenda Publishing

Agenda Publishing Limited
PO Box 185
Newcastle upon Tyne
NE20 2DH
www.agendapub.com

ISBN 978-1-78821-727-9

British Library Cataloguing-in-Publication Data
A catalogue record for this book is available from the British Library

Typeset by JS Typesetting Ltd, Porthcawl, Mid Glamorgan
Printed and bound in the UK by 4edge

Contents

Preface

Nudging is a subtle, but surprisingly controversial, technique for changing people's behaviours. This may seem like an unusual time to write a book about nudging. The formal practices of nudging have been around for over a decade (they have been informally present for much, much longer). "Nudge Units" and associated initiatives have been established in over a hundred states and nudges are an accepted part of the policy world. Despite being well established, the value of nudging is being challenged from various perspectives. Some question whether subtle nudges are up to the task of tackling the daunting global political, economic, socio-cultural and environmental challenges of our age (Pedwell 2022). Others have cast doubt on the scientific insights on which nudging is predicated. In these contexts, it is to be expected that readers may think one of two things (or maybe even two of two things): everything that needs to be said about nudging has already been articulated; and why write about something which may already be outdated?

We claim that while much has been written about the pros and cons of nudging there is significant uncertainty about its long-term prospects and direction of travel. In a recent review of nudging Ed Bradon made two interesting observations (Bradon 2022). First, he claimed that despite nudging's global spread, nudging-related practices are still relatively underutilized policy tools. Bradon estimates that an average-sized national government which mobilized nudging across all of its departments and policy regimes could be expected to deploy 6,000 nudges. He contrasts this to the 165 nudge trials that have so far been developed in two of the most prominent nudge units in the United States. Second, he claims that approximately 80 per cent of attempts to change people's behaviours, or reform organizational practices, fail. In this context Bradon argues, "Nudges are a valuable, modestly resourced and […] dramatically underused way of improving people's lives. Abandoning them now would be like discovering Aspirin then immediately shutting down production because it doesn't cure cancer" (2022).

This book is based upon the premise that we are still in the relatively early phases of the use and development of nudging, and that the future is likely to be characterized by significant innovation and change (some of it good, some of it not so good) in the use of this policy tool. We thus offer a review of the road that has so far been travelled as a basis for speculating on (and may be even modestly shaping) what the future may hold.

In undertaking this endeavour, we are keen to position ourselves as neither advocates of nudging nor cynics. Our previous research and writing on the science and practices of nudging argues that current work in the field tends to be characterized by two groups (see Jones *et al.* 2013; Whitehead *et al.* 2018). First, are those in favour of nudging. This group argue that it is a powerful and influential policy tool, which only raises fairly minor ethical and political issues. Second, are those who are suspicious of nudging. This group tends to question the influence which is often attributed to nudging (arguing that it is actually a fairly insignificant area of policy development), but, at the same time, suggest it raises troubling constitutional and ethical concerns. Rather than seeing ourselves as somewhere in the middle of these differing perspectives, we propose a third position. What if nudging is both more significant than its critics acknowledge and raises more issues than its advocates suggest?

In this book we look back over the past 12 years to consider what lessons from the early history of nudging could usefully inform its future. We also consider the role that nudging could play in helping us tackle a series of emerging social, economic and environmental problems, while reflecting on the political and ethical issues it could also generate. A particular focus in this volume is the increasingly widespread use of nudging within our digital lives. This is an area of nudging that is likely to drive the growing prevalence of nudging in our everyday actions. It is also an area that tends to be associated with the escalation of both the benefits and problems that nudging can generate. We also draw attention to the different forms that nudging can take and how these varied forms raise distinctive advantages and complications. Note, however, this volume is not a "how to" guide for nudging. Although we do reflect on the operation and effects of nudges in the real world, this book is best thought of as a guide to *what nudging actually is, where it has come from, whether we should use it, and, if so, precisely where and when is it best applied.*

We would like to acknowledge the support and inspiration of our colleagues in the Department of Geography and Earth Sciences at Aberystwyth University, and members of the Aberystwyth Behavioural Insights Interdisciplinary Research Centre. We would also like to thank Jessica Pykett, Marc Welsh, Rachel Lilley, Martin Burgess, Sandy Stevens and Joram Feitsma who we have worked with on nudge-related research over the past ten years. Finally, we would like to thank the Leverhulme Trust, the Economic and Social Research Council, the Welsh Government and the Independent Social Research Foundation for providing funding support for our research on the impacts of nudging.

1

Nudging: a gentle form of power

"Politics, in essence, is a competition between partial truths …"
Cowley (2017: 11)

According to Google's English Dictionary, the action of nudging is to "prod (somebody) gently with one's elbow to attract attention" or "to coax or gently encourage (someone) to do something". In everyday life nudging is thus synonymous with genteel actions of social notification and encouragement. Although gentle, and often innocuous, nudging is actually a powerful way to exert social influence. In his influential 1936 book *How to Win Friends and Influence People*, Dale Carnegie reveals the operational logics and power of social nudges. According to Carnegie, the key to long-term social influence is not to be found in aggressive coercion but in a deep understanding of human nature and interpersonal relations. Carnegie's central insight was that all people want to feel important. So, the key to lasting social influence was not to force people into behaving in certain ways, but to make them feel significant and valued. Carnegie advocated a series of genteel actions to promote change in others: showing sincere appreciation towards other people; demonstrating an interest in the needs and desires of others; recognizing your own mistakes before drawing people's attention to their own errors; constructing reputations for people that they will want to live up to; and even doing something as simple as remembering other people's names. There was no science behind Carnegie's insights. His philosophy of gentle social influence was derived from his experience as a salesman and public speaker. Carnegie did not use the term nudging to describe his techniques. However, as we shall see, his ideas reflect early iterations of the practices of nudging that we aim to explore in this book.

Few of us enjoy forcing people to do things. The appeal of Carnegie's insights lie in the fact that they suggest that subtle persuasion is both a more socially agreeable and often more effective way to shape the behaviours of those around us than coercion. In addition to their effectiveness, the forms of subtle persuasion promoted by Carnegie carry with them a kind of moral virtue. They suggest that one of the best ways of achieving our goals may be found in being nice to others. The forms of nudging we explore in this book are related to these everyday expressions of social influence and they are, often, associated with virtuous intentions. But they are also distinct. They are distinct because they embody a form of gentle power which has been uncovered and formally codified within various branches of the social, psychological and behavioural sciences. They are also distinct because they embody a collective orchestration of gentle forms of power by governments, corporations and NGOs to address a range of social problems. Consequently, although the forms of nudging we are interested in may be gentle, and socially sensitive, they have proven to be consequential and controversial.

We understand nudging, in its contemporary manifestations at least, as a novel science of social influence. In their definitive text on the matter, *Nudge: Improving Decisions About Health Wealth and Happiness* (2008), Richard Thaler and Cass Sunstein define a nudge as an intervention that: "[…] alters people's behaviour in a predictable way without forbidding any options or significantly changing their economic incentives" (2008: 8). There are two important dimensions of this quote. First, is the reference to predictability. Nudging draws on the insights of the behavioural and psychological sciences to suggest that it is possible to anticipate when people are likely to make bad decisions and to know how best to correct them. Now, of course, the insights of the psychological and behavioural sciences significantly predate the modern practices of nudging. As a science, psychology has consistently revealed the varied factors that contribute to human misperception and behavioural pathology (Rose 1997). But, for much of the twentieth century, psychoanalysis has suggested that human behaviour can be regulated by careful reflection on our self and associated therapeutic techniques (Nolan 1999). However, the psychological and behavioural sciences associated with nudging suggest that there may be limitations in people's abilities to effectively self-regulate their irrational actions. The second important aspect of this quote is the fact that nudging does not seek to *forbid* behaviours. As a gentle form of power, nudging avoids the use of force or financial incentives and questions the value of education to influence behaviour. Instead nudging seeks to make socially beneficial forms of behaviour easier to perceive and to achieve. On these terms nudging is, perhaps, best thought of as a project that utilizes the power of psychological and behavioural influence within free societies (see Whitehead *et al.* 2018). In other words, nudging aims to reach that elusive goal of achieving social influence while preserving personal freedom.

Interestingly, the emergence of nudging towards the end of the first decade of the twenty-first century corresponds with a period of significant political, economic and intellectual upheaval. The global financial crisis of 2007–08, and the ensuing Great Recession, mark an important hinge of history. Prior to this time the prevailing political and economic orthodoxy (neoliberalism) suggested that human nature was far too complex to understand and predict (certainly at large scales) (Binkley 2009). According to influential economists such as Friedrich Hayek, Milton Friedman and Frank Knight, the best way of balancing social stability and human freedom was not by exerting social influence (no matter how gentle), but by using systems of market exchange. The financial crisis and Great Recession understandably cast significant doubt on this worldview (see Akelof & Schiller 2009). People started to question why, if markets worked so efficiently, do they consistently generate turmoil and social crises? Furthermore, if the financial crisis was linked to errant behaviours in the financial markets would it not be a good idea to try and understand those behaviours better and regulate them more effectively? And so it was that in the wake of the Great Recession Thaler and Sunstein's book *Nudge* appeared almost as if on cue. The book was premised on the insight that not only did humans struggle to be the rational actors that economists assumed but that they were consistently irrational (see Ariely 2009).

In reality, the ideas that informed Thaler and Sunstein's book had been formulating since at least the 1940s. These ideas were often rejected by mainstream economics and maintained only a foothold in academia through their association with allied social science subjects such as psychology and administration studies (see Jones *et al.* 2013; Whitehead *et al.* 2018). But, most amazingly of all, what nudge appeared to offer was not just a basis for diagnosing the causes of various socio-economic problems (including the financial crisis) but practical, easy to follow solutions. In *Nudge* Thaler and Sunstein outline a new programme for liberal government and responsible social influence at just the moment when the world appeared desperate for better systems of social organization.

One of the most striking aspects of nudging as a policy tool is the speed of its spread. Indeed, it is difficult to think of a policy mechanism that has globalized as quickly as nudging (see Whitehead *et al.* 2014). Two of the first countries to seize on its potential were the United States and the United Kingdom. In the US the incoming Obama administration of 2009 was keen to embrace new policy approaches that could help them tackle the myriad socio-economic and environmental problems of the time. It was in this context that Barack Obama appointed Cass Sunstein as head of the Office of Information and Regulatory Affairs (see Sunstein 2013). Sunstein essentially became Obama's "nudger-in-chief". In the UK in 2010 the recently elected coalition government of David Cameron embraced nudging as a new policy orthodoxy and established one of the first designated nudge units in the world: the Behavioural Insights Team (see Halpern 2016). In one of our own studies, we discovered that by 2013 there was evidence of nudge-type policies in 136 countries, of which 51 states had centrally directed policy initiatives that appeared to be influenced by nudging practices (Whitehead *et al.* 2014). We shall consider the reasons for the popularity of nudging in Chapter 2, but one of the causes of its rapid globalization was its endorsement by a series of prominent international organizations. Between 2010 and 2018, the World Bank, OECD, United Nations and the European Commission all published reports and articles exploring and endorsing the use of nudging in a range of policy contexts, ranging from fertiliser use among impoverished farmers to the promotion of greater integrity within public life. It is clear that, outside of authoritarian states, nudging has cross-cultural appeal. It has been used to support organ donation programmes in Israel, Guatemalan tax initiatives, Medicare reform in the US, vaccine promotion in Lebanon, social housing programmes in the Netherlands, and public hygiene reform in Singapore (to name but a few examples).

There is, however, something peculiar about nudging. Even following its rapid geographical spread and clear popularity its presence may be hidden to us. In this context, it is helpful to introduce some practical examples of nudging. The following lists some prominent nudges and how they operate:[1]

---

1   These examples have mainly been drawn from two very helpful nudging databases: "A Database of 100 Nudge Case Studies and Research Papers" produced by Rohit Kaul and "Nudge Database 1.2" produced by Mark Egan at the Sterling Behavioural Science Centre.

- *Priming honesty.* People are increasingly being asked by corporations and government agencies to sign at the beginning of self-disclosure forms (perhaps for car or health insurance policies) rather than at the end. This has been proven to increase levels of honesty as it introduces the question of ethics earlier in the form-filling process. The promotion of social honesty and integrity has proven to be a prominent field of application for nudges. The subtleties of nudging appear to support the promotion of integrity more effectively than strict regulation which tends to inhibit expressions of moral virtue (it never feels particularly virtuous to be forced to do something).
- *Mandating choice.* Nations like England now use a mandated choice system for their organ donor register. When applying for a new driving licence citizens must choose whether they wish to join the register or not. No pressure is applied to the choice, but these systems provide a convenient prompt to make the decision and make the process of choosing to donate your organs after death easier.
- *Defaults and automatic escalation.* Many pension schemes now have inbuilt defaults, which assume that you wish to automatically increase your contributions as your salary rises. The default can be easily rejected by the pension scheme holder, but it means that individuals do not have to remember to increase their contributions every time they have a pay rise.
- *Social norms.* Some tax authorities send messages to citizens establishing payment compliance norms. These messages may, for example, state "nine out of ten people pay their taxes on time". These nudges have been designed to activate our desire to conform to social norms.
- *Portion sizes.* In order to prevent the overconsumption of unhealthy foods and drinks (particularly fatty foods and sugary drinks) there have been moves to reduce portion sizes. In New York City a related policy saw a proposed ban on super-sized portions of soda drinks (this was known as the sugary drink portion cap rule). The so-called "soda ban" did not prevent consumers buying two drinks that were together the same size as a super-size portion, but sought to make it appear less socially acceptable to do so.
- *Choice architecture.* In order to tackle the health problems of excessive salt consumption, restaurants in Argentina removed salt dispensers from their tables. Customers could ask for salt to be delivered to their

tables at no extra cost. This nudge did not stop people using salt, it simply made it more difficult to acquire it in the layout of a restaurant.

As far as we are aware, we have experienced four of these nudges in our everyday lives. In constructing this list, however, we must admit to being a little disingenuous. One of these actions is not really a nudge. It has been argued that the change in portion sizes in the sale of soda drinks in New York is not technically nudging. It is not a nudge because unlike the soft power of nudges it sought to regulate and ultimately ban the portion sizes associated with soft drinks. But this is where the definition of nudging becomes challenging. In the case of New York's super-size soda ban, this act of public policy clearly sought to act on the behavioural insights that nudging is based upon: namely that people find it hard to resist the temptation to make unhealthy decisions. It also sought to use the power of subtle social influence. Ordering one super-sized drink may seem socially acceptable (it is, after all, a menu option), but ordering two regular-sized drinks to consume on your own may seem a little unusual. The super-sized policy is perhaps best thought of a form of hybrid nudge. It is hybrid to the extent that it combines the psychological insights and techniques of nudging with a regulatory ban.

Ultimately, New York's soda nudge (or non-nudge, or hybrid nudge) was short lived. Following opposition from the soft drinks industry the New York Court of Appeals ruled that in imposing the rule the New York Board of Health had exceeded the limits of its powers. But the case is nonetheless a salutary lesson for this book. It reveals some of the definitional challenges associated with what nudging actually involves. In later chapters we shall consider in greater detail what counts as nudging and what does not, and why there appears to be so much confusion around the term. In this current context, we shall examine how nudge-related policies have sometimes sullied the reputation of more authentic nudges and also how, through association, nudges have at times served to place limits on the wider application of the behavioural and psychological sciences within public policy (Lowenstein & Chater 2017). The sugary drink portion cap rule also reveals the often-surprising levels of controversy that surround nudge-type policies. The super-size ban resulted in tens of thousands of written and oral comments being submitted to the New York Board of Health, both supporting and opposing the policy. Although nudges may seem gentle and in the public interest, they are normally accompanied by all kinds of complaints and concerns. In the UK the proposed use of nudges led to a House of Lords Inquiry into the political and ethical implications of related policy techniques (House of Lords 2011). In the remainder of this chapter we consider

Figure 1.1 Sign protesting against limits on soft drink size placed on a delivery truck by New York's Pepsi bottlers.

Source: The All-Nite Images. Creative Common License: https://creativecommons.org/licenses/by-sa/2.0/deed.en

why nudging is often seen as a controversial policy option and the precise nature of the complaints that are made against it. We start, however, by offering some definitional clarification of what nudging involves.

Many of the examples of nudging we have so far discussed may seem innocuous. But it is important not to underestimate their power. Nudges have been linked to billions of dollars of additional contributions to pension schemes around the world and millions of more people now being on organ donor registers. To understand the spread and implications of nudging it is important to have a very clear understanding of what they actually are. As we discussed briefly above, what actually counts and does not count as a nudge can get very complicated, very quickly. As previously stated, Thaler and Sunstein (2008: 6) define a nudge as something that: "[…] alters people's behaviour in a predictable way without forbidding any options or significantly changing their economic incentives". While pithy and helpful, this definition is light on detail. As opposed to a single definition we prefer to think of nudging in relation to five characteristics. For us, nudging:

1. Tends to target human unconscious bias as both a source of behavioural error and route to effective behavioural modification;
2. Is based upon a more-than-rational account of the human subject;
3. Offers alternative policy mechanisms to those traditionally associated with education, taxation and regulation;
4. Offers new opportunities for intervention within areas of personal wellbeing;
5. Avoids coercive measures.

It is instructive to briefly consider each of these features in turn.

One of the key insights on which nudging is based is the fact that human decision-making is informed by a range of unconscious biases (also known as heuristics) (Thaler & Sunstein 2008: 17–39). While these biases are inevitable, and sometimes even helpful, they can also lead to errors in judgement and poor long-term decision-making. Psychologists and behavioural scientists have now diagnosed hundreds of unconscious biases.[2] The biases most commonly targeted by nudges are "present bias", "status quo bias" and

---

2 The Decision Lab offer a fairly comprehensive list of such biases, with detailed explanations; see https://thedecisionlab.com/biases.

"social norms bias". Present bias occurs when we prioritize our short-term needs over a consideration of longer-term requirements. This bias is often associated with poor financial planning for our future. Status quo bias refers to the human tendency to base our next decision on our previous one in a given action space. This is why we don't tend to change mobile phone service providers, banks, or our energy tariffs even when such changes may bring improvements in our terms of service. Social norms bias (also referred to as herd instinct) relates to the human tendency to follow the behaviours of those around us. If lost in a building, trying to find a meeting room, a common course of action in this situation is to follow a person, or group of people, who appear to know where they are going – they often don't, but this reflects the operation of social norms. We use all these biases all of the time, and usually without thinking about it. They reflect shortcuts to making decisions in suboptimal conditions. Rather than ignoring these biases nudging embraces them. Nudging recognizes that it is intrinsic to the human condition to have limited amounts of time, incomplete knowledge, and a lack of cognitive capacity. We are thus not able to routinely make the correct decisions. In these situations we fall back on some simple rules of thumb: what do I need right now? What did I do in this situation last time? Or what are those around me doing? These behavioural instincts are part of our evolutionary psychology: our best chance of staying alive in early periods of human history probably depended on prioritizing present needs, following long-established behavioural routines, and staying firmly in the herd. But in the modern world these biases can lead to poor decision-making that can have deleterious consequences for our personal and collective wellbeing.

It is important to state that nudging, and nudgers, see behavioural biases as a common feature of the human condition, which afflict experts and policy-makers just as much as ordinary citizens. To take one example, while we were writing this book the former UK Chancellor of the Exchequer Kwasi Kwarteng appeared to have been afflicted by a behavioural heuristic known as an "action bias". An action bias occurs when we assume that taking some form of action to address a problem will inevitably be better than doing nothing at all. In launching his radical economic plan (or "mini-budget") in September 2022 Kwarteng suggested that in the context of limited growth in the UK economy the worst thing he could do was nothing at all. Ultimately, his radical plans to cut taxes and increase government spending led to an immediate economic crisis in the UK and his sacking as Chancellor. It turned out that doing absolutely nothing would have been immeasurably better for the UK economy and Kwasi Kwarteng's career. Now you would be hard pressed to claim that Kwasi Kwarteng is not an intelligent man: he received a double first from Cambridge University, was a Kennedy Scholar at Harvard University, and completed a PhD in economic history. But it turns out that intelligence is not a defence against behavioural biases. Action bias is a common human trait because to be seen to do nothing makes one feel, understandably, that we are more vulnerable to criticism. It just happened that Kwarteng's action bias cost the UK government tens of billions of pounds.

Nudging not only recognizes the role of biases in generating behavioural problems, but also sees them as potential routes for behavioural modification. If you know that people have present bias, why not offer them a grant to install low-carbon technology (perhaps for an air source heat pump), which only has to be paid back in the longer-term future (perhaps with the energy cost savings that the technology provides)? This essentially reverses the present bias to make it work for, rather than against, action on climate change. The use of defaults (the pre-set option that is made available when we do nothing) also reflects the repurposing of a bias within the practices of nudging. If you know that people exhibit status quo bias, then resetting defaults to better serve personal and collective needs (perhaps for enhanced saving rates) would seem like a logical course of action. Once enrolled on a company pension scheme, for example, our behavioural bias towards inertia would appear to work in our own long-term interest, rather than against it.

The targeting of unconscious biases does, of course, connect to the second key characteristic of nudging identified above: namely, an interest in the "more-than-rational" nature of human subjectivity. Rational accounts of human action tend to assume key features in human decision-making: that humans have the necessary information needed to make a decision; that they have the cognitive capacity to assess the information they need to make an effective decision; that they have adequate time to make optimal decisions; that they will seek to maximize their self-interests; and that they generally act in relative social isolation. Nudging is predicated upon a much more messy account of human decision-making. This does, of course, involve recognizing the role of unconscious biases and practical shortcuts in our decision-making. But it does not suggest that all human action is purely irrational. A more-than-rational account of the human subject recognizes the interplay of deliberation and unconscious instinct. In formal terms advocates of nudging tend to employ a so-called "dual system" theory of human decision-making (Kahneman 2011). System 1 in this schema is the quicker, more automatic forms of decision-making that are associated with unconscious biases and heuristics. Whereas System 2 reflects much slower and effortful reflections on options. Nudging assumes that System 1 is the most powerful realm of human decision-making (largely because so many of the thousands of decisions we have to make every day must be made quickly). But nudgers also recognize the importance of System 2 thinking and even consider how nudging can be used to encourage greater conscious engagement with problems (John *et al.* 2011) (we shall discuss these so-called "nudge-think" approaches in Chapter 4). There is no consensus on precisely how nudge theorists understand the relationship between System 1 and System 2 thinking (Lin 2017). Nevertheless these systems provide the prevailing model of human decision-making that consistently informs the design and implementation of nudges.

The interest that nudgers have in the more-than-rational nature of human behaviour inevitably means that nudging brings into question the effectiveness of many traditional policy mechanisms. Traditional public policy takes three main forms: education, financial/taxation incentives, and legislation/regulation. Each of these domains of policy assumes a rational subject who will: (1) learn the lessons of education; (2) maximize financial incentives or minimize fiscal costs; and (3) avoid breaking the law. If we consider just one area of public policy we can see the limitations that are associated with these policy tools. In the UK, the use of hand-held mobile phones while driving has been targeted by a series of awareness-raising campaigns, financial penalties and new laws. Despite these actions tens of thousands of drivers have been guilty of mobile phone-related offences in the UK. It is not that conventional forms of policy action don't have their role, it is just that they only appeal to one part of a our decision-making system. Most likely, when people are tempted to use their mobile devices while driving they are not thinking rationally about the risks of their actions but about the excitement of receiving a new message or the need to send that urgent email. In these more emotionally charged circumstances nudging would suggest that a better way to prevent people using mobile phones would be for people to set up automatic Bluetooth lockouts on their phones, which can only be unlocked when the user is not driving.

Nudging also offers new opportunities for governmental intervention into citizen's personal lives. Historically, within liberal society a simple principle has determined the scope and limitations of state intervention into people's everyday lives. This norm is known as the "harm to others principle" (Mill 1859). The harm to others principle asserts that governments should only intervene within the lives of citizens if their actions are causing harm to others. The idea here is that governments only have the right to limit people's freedom if those freedoms are reducing the freedoms of others. This principle is why governments have generally been more active in trying to avert environmental problems (when, for example, the production of air pollution by one party adversely affects the health of another group), than in addressing the growing obesity problem (an issue which is often seen as more of a *harm to self* than a harm to others issue). Nudging challenges this orthodoxy because as a gentle form of power, which focuses on reframing choice and psychological suggestion, its advocates claim that it can be used to govern citizens' private lives without undermining their liberty. So long as nudges remain easy to resist, the argument goes, they can be used to address harm to self as well as harm to others issues.

The final characteristic of nudging relates to the aforementioned ways it seeks to expand the legitimate field of government. Since its inception, nudging has consistently sought to reduce the need for coercive forms of state intervention. By coercion we are referring to forms of paternalism that seek to forcefully determine the behaviours of citizens. In general terms paternalism involves the use of laws, regulations, and the active monitoring and policing of behaviours in much the same way a parent seeks to control the actions of their child. Nudging advocates argue that not only are such forms of paternalism costly, but they are often ineffective and have the additional cost of reducing people's freedom (Lowenstein & Chater 2017). Nudging is typically associated with *soft* paternalism: the encouragement of certain forms of behaviour you might expect to receive from an aunt or uncle, rather than an overbearing parent. Nudging is thus more aligned with an avuncular form of government than a nanny state. As such, nudging tends to appeal across the political spectrum – offering as it does the promise of an expanded scope of government intervention to those of the left, and a less coercive form of government to those of the right (Thalter & Sunstein 2008).

Throughout this book we claim that nudges are defined by each of the five characteristics outlined above, to greater or lesser extents. It is, perhaps, easiest to think of nudging in its purist form using this checklist. In the wild, however, the nature and form of nudging is less clear. The messy reality of nudging means that there is much debate about what actually counts as a nudge and what does not. The complexities associated with identifying nudges in the wild can be thought of from a variety of perspectives. For example, what precisely is the relationship between nudging and coercion? We have suggested above that it is perhaps best to think of nudging as occupying the middle ground on a spectrum between libertarianism and coercion. However, different types of nudges can be more or less libertarian or coercive in form. It is possible to argue, for example, that the use of subtle nudges in food labelling is all pretty libertarian given the fact that many people don't even look at food labels. At the other end of the spectrum, some claim that the resetting of defaults on organ donor registers or company pension schemes from opt-in to opt-out are fairly coercive (because they essentially make a decision for someone knowing full well that status quo bias and general inertia means they will not opt-out) (see Thaler & Sunstein 2022). On these terms, rather than thinking of nudges existing in a pure space of distinction somewhere between libertarianism and coercion, we argue that nudging should be seen as something of a moveable feast: oscillating between, if never fully occupying, the same space as these policy extremes.

In other contexts, it is not always clear that nudging can be separated out from financial mechanisms of behavioural modification. In 2011 Wales became one of the first countries to introduce a charge for single-use carrier bags. The introduction of a financial penalty such as this would normally be seen as very different from the soft power of nudges. However, in this case the charge for single-use carrier bags was only 5 pence. Given the minimal

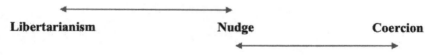

Figure 1.2 Nudging in relation to libertarianism and coercive policy measures

cost, it seems reasonable to assume that in this context an economic charge was actually being used as a nudge. The charge was easy to pay, and it could be argued that its role was not to financially disincentivize the use of plastic bags, but to change the social norm that surrounded their utilization. Of course, there is scope for the use of such financial incentives within the classic definition of a nudge: Thaler and Sunstein suggest that a nudge could still be considered a nudge so long as it did not "significantly" alter economic incentives. But the case of Wales's plastic bag charge reveals the connections that exist between nudges and more traditional policy mechanisms (particularly education, financial incentives and mandates). In certain instances nudges can inform and be part of educational programmes of behaviour change, new fiscal mechanisms of governance and even make mandates more effective. In the case of Wales, it is instructive to note that the single-use plastic-bag nudge was also a precursor to a more comprehensive ban on single-use plastics. In this context, in establishing new social norms nudges can clear the way for more substantial forms of regulation.

Throughout this book we shall explore the unique contributions that nudging can offer to public policy problems. We shall, however, remain

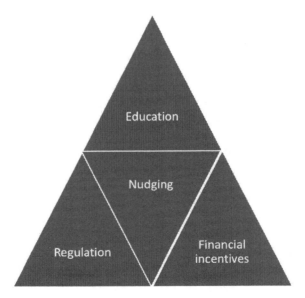

Figure 1.3 Nudging in relation to more traditional policy instruments

mindful of the various forms that nudges can take and the uncertainties that remain over what should and should not be considered a nudge. As opposed to only seeking out nudging in its purest form, we aim to explore its various influences and adaptations in the wild, and to consider the relative pros and cons of actually existing nudges.

As we consider the development and application of nudges in the real world it will become clear that nudging has been deployed in three main contexts: (1) by governments to shape the behaviour of citizens; (2) within large organizations (including government departments and corporations) in order to shape their operations; and (3) by corporations to change the behaviours of consumers. At the centre of many of the most vociferous concerns about nudging is the idea that it reflects a form of mass psychological manipulation which we are powerless to resist. This kind of "psych-ops" critique suggests that nudging embodies the orchestration of psychological power by governments and/or corporations and is contrary to the very nature of democratic politics. In other words, nudging is seen by some as a form socio-psychological control, which is not subject to the same forms of democratic scrutiny that are given to laws and mandates. The UK's House of Lords inquiry into nudging asserted that in order to conform to democratic requirements nudges should be open to human discernment, political discussion and contestation (House of Lords 2011).

In the context of the numerous expressions of authoritarian violence and oppression and anti-democratic popularism evident around the world today, these critiques of nudging may seem a little heavy handed. But nudging does present some uncomfortable challenges to the assumptions on which modern liberal democracies are based. In addition to changing what the state does and how it does certain things, nudging carries with it an inherent critique of the assumptions that are made regarding the competencies of citizens in modern democracies. It exposes the behavioural weaknesses of people and reveals the presence of psychological limitations to their intentional capacities. Nudging is seen by some as embodying a post-enlightenment vision of the modern citizen: one that not only recognizes the limitations of *Homo economicus*, but which suggests that some of these limitations are inherent to the human condition (Whitehead *et al.* 2017). In suggesting that governments can legitimately intervene in the everyday lives of citizens – in order to make people's lives consistently healthier and wealthier – nudging has also been associated with the potential erosion of tolerance

(Furedi 2011a). Tolerance towards alternative ways of living is a central pillar of liberal democracies. In offering a behavioural prognosis of social ills, and a softly paternalistic route to addressing related problems, nudging has been associated with an intolerant attitude to errant lifestyles. In this context nudging could easily become a tool for the exercise of a form of "tyranny of the majority"-perspective on what constitutes the good life. In his fascinating review of modern state theory *Confronting Leviathan* (2021) David Runciman argues that politics emerges out of the distinction and relationships between rulers and the ruled. He also claims that modern states are neither principalities or republics – they are, in fact, both. In this context, we should not be surprised that despite being a distinctly gentle form of power nudging should have been so politically controversial. Whatever its moral implications, nudging unquestionably disrupts established relationships between the rulers and the ruled and shakes the kaleidoscope of republican and princely forms of power in the modern state.

A final set of critiques that have been raised against nudging relate to their efficacy (see Bradon 2022). Despite the various claims that are made about the public policy successes of nudging, some have questioned whether too much is being claimed about the power of nudging (Jones *et al.* 2013). These critiques tend to fall into two categories. First are those which suggest that nudges are too small, and too gentle to address the complex challenges being faced by governments and people around the world. For example, Lowenstein and Chater (2017) argue that nudging focuses too much on individual decision-making and not the structural nature of socio-economic problems. They use the case of obesity in the US and ask whether elevated rates of obesity in that country can really be linked to particularly high levels of behavioural biases in that population, or whether they are more likely a product of the nature of the nation's political economy. Others, however, argue that nudging is not small enough (Bradon 2022). In focusing on citizens' immediate choice environment nudging does not seek to educate or change the values and outlook of citizens. While this may appeal to libertarian norms, it is claimed that it is unlikely to produce long-term patterns of behaviour change (see Crompton 2010).

Critiques of nudging generally fall into three categories: ethics (that is their impacts on the constitutional norms of government in free societies); empowerment (the impact of nudging on personal freedom and autonomy); and efficacy (does nudging actually work) (see Jones *et al.* 2013). We shall explore these "three Es" in greater depth in later chapters. Central to our argument will be the notion that many of these critiques embody overreactions to what are fairly helpful, well-intentioned and benign policy interventions. But we shall argue that with the rising use of digital (hyper-)nudging by corporations on smart devices and social media platforms these critiques start to become more pertinent. Ultimately, we claim nudging is significant not just because of the initiatives it has spawned, but because it has provided a context for thinking in new ways about public policy and the governing of various socio-economic problems. We started this chapter with a quote from Jason Cowley: "politics, in essence, is a competition between partial truths ...". In the remainder of this volume we consider the partial truths that nudging reveals about the human condition, while also considering the inevitable limitations and blind spots of its associated views of the world.

2

Histories of nudging

"No predicament is so bleak as to be unimprovable by historical investigation into its origins and development"

Smith (2022: 56)

It is, perhaps, unfair to characterize nudging as a predicament. In keeping with Justin Smith, however, we do believe that in order to improve the use and application of nudging in the future it is vital to have a sound understanding of its past. Several accounts exist of the history of nudging and its foundational ideas. These histories have been developed both by advocates of nudging (see Hallsworth & Kirkman 2020; Oliver 2017; Thaler 2016; Sunstein 2013) and by those adopting more critical perspectives (see Jones *et al.* 2013; Whitehead *et al.* 2018). In this chapter we do not seek to merely repeat these stories. Instead, by charting the intertwining histories of the ideas, institutions and practices that have contributed to the emergence of nudging we aim to reveal why nudging has taken the forms it has, why there are evident variations in the ways it is understood and applied, and how in the future nudging may take very different forms. In this context, the value of an historical perspective on nudging lies in the fact that it can help to reveal the inherent *contingency of the present* and open-up new futures.

Figure 2.1 indicates the rising popularity of "nudging" as an internet search term since the publication of Thaler and Sunstein's *Nudge* in the spring of 2008. There is a fairly steady rise in interest in the term over the next 7 years or so until a marked peak in 2017. This is clearly the historical watershed for the term. So, what happened in 2017? In 2017 Richard Thaler, the first author of *Nudge* and Professor of Behavioural Science and Economics at the University of Chicago received the Nobel Memorial Prize in Economic Sciences for his contributions to behavioural economics and media and web interest in the idea of nudging naturally spiked following the announcement of the award. But this point in time is a salutary one from which to work back from in our exploration of the history of nudging. It is important because it reveals how nudging (or at least the scientific ideas on which it is based) had by this point become a matter of scientific and political orthodoxy. As we shall see, for much of its pre-history (before 2008) nudging and its underlying sciences had been on the periphery of the scientific and policy mainstream. The 2017 Nobel Prize is a significant point in the history of nudging because it reveals the undeniable significance of the concept (and its underlying science). In his "banquet speech" at the award ceremony, Thaler discussed his body of scholarship alongside the work of other Nobel Laureates whose work had revealed "colliding blackholes" and "genes that know the time of day" (Thaler 2017). While acknowledging that these comparisons were daunting, Thaler wryly noted how "I discovered the presence of human life, in a place not far far away, in a place where my fellow economists thought it did not exist – the economy" (Thaler 2017). The history of nudging is first and foremost a history of the discovery of life in the economy, or more accurately in the economic sciences. It is also a history of the emergence of a more complex understanding of people, and their behavioural motivations, by policymakers.

The history of nudging, we argue, can be broken down into four broad time periods (see Figure 2.2 below). In this chapter we shall focus on the three periods that lead up to Richard Thaler's Nobel Prize in 2017.

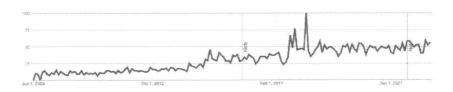

Figure 2.1 Interest in the internet search term "nudging" 2008–22 (Google Trends)

Note: Numbers on Y-axis reflect interest in term relative to a maximum interest of 100, which denotes the peak of popularity for a search term.

A Pre-history of nudging

From bounded rationality to heuristics, 1945–70

There is a history of nudging that predates its naming and codification by Thaler and Sunstein in 2008. A key starting point of this pre-history is the pioneering work of the American social scientist Herbert Simon. In many ways social scientist is a misnomer when it comes to Simon. His work spanned the social sciences but also incorporated mathematics and computer sciences. It is thus of note that in addition to winning the Nobel Memorial Prize in Economic Sciences (1978) he also received the Turing Award for his work in the field of computing. In his early work Simon was interested in administrative behaviour and the ways in which individuals act when working within organizations. He was particularly concerned with the types of organizational behaviours that did not confirm with rational models of economics and resulted in dysfunctional organizations. Many of Simon's key insights and theories were expressed in his 1947 book *Administrative Behaviour* (Simon 1997). Based on Simon's doctoral research, this is one of the founding texts of nudging even though it does not use the term.

Administrative Behaviour offers a microeconomic account of the decision-making processes deployed by administrators. In order to make sense of these decisions Simon recognized that he needed more than the theories of rational utility maximization common in economics: he also needed accounts of cognition and behavioural motivation that were associated with psychology. Simon's fusion of economics and psychology resulted in an account of the limits to human rationality and the strategies that are used to work with these limitations when making a decision. In *Administrative Behaviour* Simon used the term "limits of rationality" to describe the constraints of human decision-making. In his 1957 book *Models of Man* he used the now more familiar term of "bounded rationality". Simon's work revealed two main sets of bounds that are placed on every human decision. First, there are the limits of the environment (or organization) in which we make a decision. Simon recognized that it was rare for an environment to furnish us with all the information that was needed to make an optimal decision. Second, there are the limits of human cognition. Even if we had all of the available information we needed to make the best decision Simon

Figure 2.2 Key periods in the history of nudging

recognized that we lack the time and cognitive bandwidth to be able to consistently make optimal decisions.

Simon developed an interesting way to visualize his notion of bounded rationality. He likened human decision-making to a pair of scissors (see Figure 2.3). In Simon's visual model one blade of the scissors is human cognition (this could also be referred to as the mind, see Lockton 2012). The other blade represents the decision-making context (or environment). According to Simon, human behaviour occurs at the intersection of mind and environment. Each cut of the scissors is a decision/action that combines a cognitive act with a contextual situation. The cut in the paper is always made by the blades coming together. For example, our decision of what to eat during an evening meal is, in part, driven by the cognitive calculations that go into our assessment of food (reading the menu, remembering previous occasions we have tried the different dishes on offer, thinking about what we have eaten earlier in the day, considering the health benefits or costs of certain foods, deciding on whether we want to eat meat or not, etc.). But the decision is also conditioned by our context (e.g. eating meat when out with a group of vegetarians may seem insensitive, our ability to calorie count may be restricted by the restaurant not including calorific information on the menu). We may not be sure precisely how the coming together of cognition and context shape our final culinary decision but Simon argues that we can be sure they do. In addition to providing us with a helpful model of the complexities of our decision-making, Simon's scissors also demonstrate the nature of bounded rationality. Each decision-making cut will inevitably be defined by limitations in both our cognitive capacity and the decision-making environment. As we shall see, the connections between cognition and context are central to the nudging project and its emphasis on cognitive biases and choice architecture.

Simon's work introduced an additional concept in and through which to understand and interpret bounded rationality. According to Simon, human decisions are characterized by a process of "satisficing". Satisficing suggests the primacy of coming to a satisfactory decision as opposed to an optimal one. While classical economics suggests that we utilize knowledge and wise judgement to make the best possible decision, Simon argues that it is more common for us to simply choose the first option that comes close to our expectations. One way we can think of satisficing is through the example of getting married or selecting a life partner. In addition to our inability to be able to date a suitable sample size of people to make a statistically reliable judgement about who would be our best partner, it is unlikely that potential partners will wait around while we determine that they are actually a suitable match. So, what do we do? Typically, we see which potential partners come our way and hope that the first one we meet who we think we would like to spend the rest of our lives with feels the same way (romantic, we know!). Of course, online dating platforms, with their machine learning and algorithms, promise us more optimized ways of selecting partners, but for many the single most important decision of our lives is an outcome of satisficing.

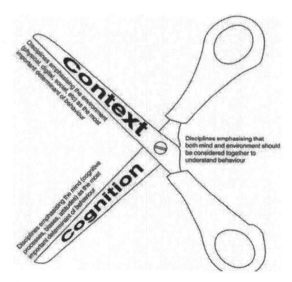

Figure 2.3 Hebert Simon's behavioural scissors
Source: Lockton (2012).

There are two aspects of Simon's life and career which are rarely acknowledged. The first is that despite the theoretical focus of his work, he did attempt to apply his insights into organizational decision-making in practical contexts. In 1948 he helped to create the Economic Cooperation Administration: the organization that was responsible for delivering US aid in the form of the Marshall Plan to Western Europe after the Second World War (Lindbeck 1992). He also served on the President's Science Advisory Committee in the Johnson and Nixon administrations. It is difficult to know precisely how Simon and his theories of decision-making influenced the working of these organizations, but his work therein most probably reflects the first policy impacts of nudge-related ideas. The second overlooked aspect of his life is the potential influence of his wife on his thinking.[1] Dorothea Pye Simon met Herbert Simon at the University Chicago in the 1930s. Pye Simon studied political science and completed her graduate studies on the factors determining successful forms of urban management.[2] Later in life Pye Simon began research in cognitive psychology and became interested in patterns of learning among young children. This led to her becoming involved in a joint study (and publication) with Herbert Simon into the nature of spelling errors among children. It is difficult to determine the extent to which Pye Simon's work and experience influenced the thinking of her husband. Given Pye Simon's work on the operation of large urban administrations and her later concern with human error, we think it inconceivable that she did not have some influence on Simon's work. While we may never know for sure, she most likely played some role in the development of the ideas and principles that would lead to nudging.

Kahneman's scissors: the rise of behavioural economics

The next significant phase in the development of ideas associated with nudging arrived in the 1970s. Working at the interface of economics and

---

1   Most histories of nudging tell the tale of white, European men. Although it would be impossible to recount the history of nudging without acknowledging the prominent role of men, throughout this book we seek to emphasize the important part played by women in this history.

2   See "Biography – 'Dorothea Pye Simon' – Simon – Correspondence – biographies (literary works)", Carnegie Mellon University Digital Collections; https://digital collections.library.cmu.edu/node/36628.

psychology, Daniel Kahneman and Amos Tversky sought to better understand how humans made decisions under the forms of limitations outlined by Simon (see Lewis 2017). Kahneman and Tversky wanted to know how, given the decision-making limitations reflected in Simon's scissors, humans actually made decisions in conditions of uncertainty. They essentially asked the question: if we always cut imperfectly what guides do we use to determine when and how to cut? Kahneman and Tversky's work was original for two main reasons. First, because it rejected the use of idealized models of human rational behaviour (which were the mainstay of economics) as reliable proxies for human action. Second, because they studied human decision-making on the basis of errors. This shift from assumed human competence to a study of human mistakes was revolutionary. It was revolutionary because it changed the default of social science inquiry from one of assumed perfection to presumed error.

There were two underlying suppositions in Kahneman and Tversky's research. The first was a belief that in the context of imperfect knowledge and uncertainty (identified by Simon) humans relied on mental models which could be used to make sense of the world. In lay terms we would probably call these mental models intuition. The second was an assumption that these mental models were not random but were regularly and consistently deployed by all manner of people. In order to test these assumptions Kahneman and Tversky were faced with a problem: how do you study errors and mistakes? They realized that in order to test the nature of error, you had to first create situations that would deliberately induce it. One of their earliest techniques was asking school children questions which they did not have the necessary information to answer accurately (Lewis 2017). The hope was that by inducing errors they could see if study participants deployed mental models when making real-world decisions. They essentially hoped to see whether error was systemic in human decision-making.

Kahneman and Tversky's study of induced error lead in 1974 to the publication of a paper in the journal *Science* under the innocuous title of "Judgment under Uncertainty: Heuristics and Biases" (Kahneman & Tversky 1974). This paper offered empirical evidence of the systemic nature of bias in human decision-making. This paper would ultimately lead to the pair's most influential idea: "prospect theory" (or what is now more commonly referred to as loss aversion). Prospect theory argued that humans felt the pain of a loss much more than the joy of a gain (Kahneman & Tversky

1979). According to the theory, people would be much more averse to losing $1,000 than they value gaining it. In classic economic terms $1,000 is always $1,000 (no more and no less) and there should be no expectation that we would assess the loss and gain of this amount of money as different amounts. Michael Lewis provocatively described prospect theory as "[…] a truck packed with psychology that might be driven into the inner sanctums of economics and exploded" (2017: 284). In reality, the fuse of the explosive proved to be quite long, and prospect theory did not really disrupt economic orthodoxies until the early years of the new millennium. It is interesting to consider what enabled prospect theory to disrupt our understanding of the human condition in ways that Herbert Simon's work never quite managed.

Apparently, Daniel Kahneman is quite a messy and disorganized person (see Lewis 2017). His level of disorganization led to his assistant attaching a piece of string to his office scissors and tying it to his chair. We mention this here because we find it somewhat amusing that Simon's metaphorical scissor-based representation of human limitations took a literal scissor-based form for Kahneman. We also mention it because despite his disorganized nature Kahneman recognized the value of rigorous empirical studies. Some of his early work was based upon laboratory-based studies of how the human eye responds to light signals (*ibid.*). This commitment to scientific methods appears to have been central to the acceptance of Kahneman and Tversky's early work. Their research not only brought into question the assumptions of economic models, it also challenged many of the political, legal and ethical notions of human rights and responsibilities that had been established in the wake of the Enlightenment. If humans are systematically biased and prone to poor decision-making, think of the implications for elections, political participation and legal responsibility? Empirical scientific evidence was Kahneman's and Tversky's silver bullet. It is what enabled them to both publish their work in economics journals in the 1970s and what would eventually enable their ideas (through the practices of nudging) to gain political acceptance in the twenty-first century (Hallsworth & Kirkman 2020: 31).

There is one final implication of Kahneman and Tvesky's work that is important to raise: their understanding of error. Despite owing a debt to psychological research, their view of human error is both peculiarly immutable and inherently economic in its orientation. The immutability of the forms of human error identified by Kahneman and Tversky has been most clearly articulated in some of Kahneman's most recent work (Tversky died in 1996), and in his alignment with dual-system theories of human decision-making. As we discussed in Chapter 1, Kahneman and Tversky's theories of human bias and error are generally connected to a broader theory of "fast" (System 1) and "slow" (System 2) thinking. Biases derive from our need to make many quick, unconscious and often automatic decisions. While Kahneman acknowledges our capacity for more deliberative slow thinking, he argues that System 1 is king. Despite emerging evidence to the contrary, Kahneman argues that we have too many decisions to make, and that our biases are too ingrained, for us to realistically use System 2 to control System 1 thinking. Despite emerging from psychological insights into human decision-making, Kahneman and Tversky's notion of error is also characterized by an economic orientation. It essentially identifies and defines error in relation to divergencies in behaviour from the expectation of rational economic theory. This is a peculiar perspective because it seeks to challenge the orthodoxies of economic models of human action only to reinstate them as the normative model against which to measure deviance (see Jones *et al.* 2013). Many psychologists do not recognize the biases that Kahneman and Tversky uncovered as errors because, unlike in theories of rational economic action, they do not have an agreed upon sense of normal human behaviour (Hallsworth & Kirkman 2020: 39). After all, you can only observe an error if there is a correct response to compare it with. Certain psychologists and behavioural scientists have also challenged Kahneman and Tversky's derogatory characterization of bias as errors. Gerd Gigerenzer has, for example, recognized the value of automatic forms of decisions as effective and efficient forms of action when they are used in appropriate contexts (Gigerenzer 2015).[3]

---

3 Gigerenzer and his collaborators describe how they have developed a simple heuristic framework to assist doctors who have to quickly decide whether to refer patients to specialist cardiology units or to regular beds (quite literally life and death decisions). Gigerenzer argues that well-designed heuristic devices (in this context three simple questions) produce more effective results in medical decision-making than more complex assessment procedures (see https://www.youtube.com/watch?v=9H_R9gssjuI). So decision-making shortcuts are not intrinsically linked to error. This does, of course, raise the intriguing question of what the difference is between a well-designed heuristic (like Gigerezer's cardio-medical checklist) and a nudge.

The scientific categorization of human biases by Kahneman and Tversky is significant to the history of nudging for several reasons. First of all their ideas would inspire a young Richard Thaler (Thaler 2015). He, along with Kahneman, Tversky and others would establish the field of behavioural economics which would provide a key source of inspiration for nudging. Secondly, the biases that Kahneman and Tversky revealed would ultimately become both the target of nudging practices and the medium through which related interventions were delivered. Thirdly, by connecting human biases with notions of error and divergence from a rational economic norm, Kahneman and Tversky identified a pathology that nudging seeks to cure. Fourthly, and related to the previous point, by seeing System 1 biases as dominant parts of the human operating system, Kahneman and Tversky suggested that there was little point supporting people to consciously overcome their behavioural biases. Ultimately, the pioneering work of Kahneman and Tversky not only gave rise to nudging, but it critically shaped its form. As we shall see, this would result in the emergence of a dominant strand of nudging that focused on correcting behavioural bias through the use of unconscious biases.

"Mad Men" and the corporate origins of nudging

The standard story of the history of nudging locates it firmly in the work of Nobel Prize-winning academics. There is, however, a parallel history that while important is rarely acknowledged (see Whitehead *et al.* 2018: 28–33). In the postwar period (roughly between the work of Simon and Kahneman and Tversky), there were early iterations of nudging going on in the corporate world. It would be wrong to claim that nudging is just the public-sector adoption of marketing techniques. However, it is clear that early forms of psychologically attuned marketing techniques were operating in the same area of human inquiry as Simon, Kahneman and Tversky. In his classic account of the development of the modern marketing industry *The Hidden Persuaders* Vance Packard describes the coming together of intuitive forms of large-scale psychological analyses and the rise of consumer society (Packard 1957). In a telling passage in his book, Packard reflects on an emerging vision of the human subject on Maddison Avenue in the immediate postwar years:

> The typical American citizen is commonly depicted as an uncommonly shrewd person. He or she is dramatized as a thoughtful voter, rugged individualist, and, above all, as a careful hard-headed consumer [...] Typically [those in the marketing industry] see us as bundles of daydreams, misty hidden yearnings, guilt complexes, irrational emotional blockages [...] image lovers given to impulsive and compulsive acts.   (Packard 1957: 6–7)

Sound familiar? It should do. Packard is describing the distinction that Simon had already made between *Homo economicus* and actual human decision-making ten years before.

It would be wrong to suggest that what was happening in the marketing sector was a form of rigorous scientific inquiry. It is perhaps best to think of it as an emerging art rather than science of social persuasion that focused on one behaviour: consumption. It is clear, however, that through the use of clever promotional strategies (for example, the use of discount coupons) that marketing was conducting informal experiments in the field of unconscious human biases (in the context of coupons, the principle of loss aversion). Just as people lived by the rules of gravity before Sir Isaac Newton scientifically explained its existence, the marketing industry was uncovering and using as yet unnamed human behavioural traits to achieve their goals. They were essentially providing early proof-of-concept trials for as yet unidentified human behaviours. The proof of concept was confirmed through the sale, or not, of goods.

Obviously, early corporate experiments in nudging techniques did not focus on the areas of public policy concern (health, environment, financial prudence) that we now associate with nudges. Indeed, it could be argued that in promoting mass consumption that these corporate experiments were actually generating the socio-environmental problems that modern nudges are attempting to address. During the 1960s, however, an approach to policy emerged that applied corporate marketing techniques directly to public policy problems. "Social marketing" is based on the premise that it should be possible to use the power of marketing to sell things and promote practices that contribute to the common good. In this context it sought to fuse the practical insights of the marketing industry with the theoretical insights of the behavioural and social sciences in order to address collective action challenges. In its early form social marketing became a popular policy tool for the promotion of family planning and population growth control measures. An early example of such a programme was instigated in India in 1963 by the Ford Foundation and the Indian Institute of Management (see Whitehead *at al.* 2018: 30–32). This programme focused on the social promotion of condom use. Rather than promoting condoms through education and persuasion, the programme sought to market them as commercial products. Branding techniques and marketing campaigns were thus used to make the use of condoms more socially acceptable and to connect them to desired forms of lifestyle. Here we see clear links between nudging and social marketing: they both acknowledge that there is more driving the adoption of certain behaviours than merely cost and knowledge.

During the 1980s, social marketing techniques became an important tool in the fight against HIV/AIDs (UNAIDS 2000). Social marketing insights were central to attempts to move condom distribution away from healthcare facilities and clinics into everyday spaces (thus shifting what nudgers would call social norms and removing associated stigmas). Social marketing techniques have also emphasized the importance of moving away from experts and towards the use of community advocates in the field of sexual health promotion (so called community social marketing) (UNAIDS 2000: 9–10). The use of social marketing in the battle against HIV/AIDS in the 1980 and 1990s represents an important practical experiment in the power of social norms in affecting behaviour change at large scales. The use of social norms is a key feature of modern nudging, but its role in public health campaigns in the more distant pass is often overlooked within histories of nudging. This is, perhaps, a significant oversight because it hides the creative energies that were unleashed in the fight against one of the most significant health crises of the late twentieth century.

Some in the social marketing field feel that their role in the development of nudging has been overlooked and written out of associated histories. This is, in many ways, a troubling oversight. It fails to notice the significant contribution that practical experimentation in behaviour change techniques played in informally providing evidence of many of the insights that were being scientifically identified in psychological laboratories and trials. The success of social marketing techniques clearly helped to shift policy-making norms and pave the way for the adoption of nudging down the line. This oversight also tends to downplay the role of numerous NGOs and community workers in Africa, India, and South-east Asia who contributed to the field-based testing and calibration of more human-centred public policy initiatives. Acknowledging the non-Western origins of nudging, outside of formal academic institutions, does not only offer a more accurate history of nudging, it also helps to reveal the heterodox origins of nudging, which have been somewhat closed off during recent attempts to professionalize the field (Feitsma & Whitehead 2022).

In some ways, the story of the role of corporations in the history of nudging has come full circle. The science of nudging and related public policy experiments is now informing the activities of the corporate sector. A series of commercially orientated nudge units now exist (see Whitehead *et al.* 2018: 136–56). For example, Ogilvy Mather, one of the world's most prominent advertising and public relations firms, established Ogilvy Change to operationalize nudging in the corporate sector (they even have an annual conference called Nudgestock!). These units sell nudging insights to support the sales of goods and services and to help transform employee behaviours. Peter Buell Hirsch (2021) has identified a series of ways in which nudge-related insights are shaping corporate cultures, including the promotion of ethical practices, preventing groupthink, and improving health and safety measures. A particularly interesting example of the use of nudging to promote health and safety in the workplace relates to manufacturing. According to Hirsch, a common source of accidents in factories is the damage to workers' hands from fast-moving machinery. In some companies, machine workers are now required to wear gloves that have a skeletal outline of the human hand on them (see Figure 2.4). In other contexts, companies have found nudges useful behavioural tools to help them meet their regulatory duties. In the UK, following the privatization of water and energy services, many companies are subject to significant penalties if they fail to meet the standards set by regulators. Securing the continuity of supply of water and energy (and thus avoiding fines) often involves utility companies using nudges (such as energy bills that include elements of social comparison) to shape consumer behaviour and reduce consumption patterns.

There are many examples of the corporate misuse of nudges, so-called "sludges", that use the insights of the behavioural sciences and more informal commercial experiments, but do not have the individual's best interests in mind. These may be techniques to ensure that consumers keep using a service by making it much easier to sign-up than to unsubscribe (see Luo 2022) or by generating loss aversion by not revealing the full picture (e.g.

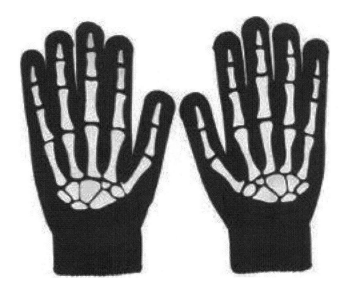

Figure 2.4 Skeletal gloves: nudging workplace safety for machine workers

hotel booking sites that prompt "there are only 4 rooms left at this hotel" while not disclosing that more rooms are available to purchase at the same hotel on other sites). There are, however, some examples of the corporate interpretation of nudging that not only seek highly ethical applications for related insights, but also offer more conceptually nuanced interpretations of how to understand and apply nudges (see Corporate Culture Group's Human Operating System framework).[4]

Ultimately, any history of nudging must acknowledge the influences it has absorbed from the corporate world. As this section has demonstrated, these influences are neither simple nor unidirectional, with corporations directly and indirectly shaping nudging techniques and nudging influencing corporate practices only to be reinterpreted and reapplied within the private sector.

---

4   The framework creatively considers the implications of the conscious and unconscious individual identified within B. F. Skinner's and Kahneman and Tversky's work. Crucially, however the framework also engages with the broader social sciences to consider the role of collective forms of conscious and unconscious actions in the corporation; see https://corporateculture.co.uk/the-human-operating-system/.

Cognitive design and engineering: from door handles to nuclear meltdowns

A final key development in the prehistory of nudging is the emergence of cognitive design and engineering (or, as it is more commonly referred to, *user-centred design*). This is a branch of design which reflects many of the observations and concerns that are evident in the work of Simon, Kahneman and Tversky concerning bounded rationality. However, while Kahneman and Tversky were primarily interested in the cognitive (human) blade of Simon's scissors, cognitive designers and engineers are more concerned with the environmental blade. In this context, cognitive designers argue that the *design environments* within which we live out our daily lives are ill fitted to effective human cognition and behaviour. These design environments include software interfaces, homes, workplaces, transport hubs, megacities, and the reported 20,000 objects we are likely to come into contact with every day (Norman 2013). Crucially, cognitive designers claim that it is changes in these environments that are central to addressing common forms of human error and poor decision-making.

A central figure in the development of cognitive design and engineering is the American academic Donald Norman. Norman's first area of academic interest focused on electrical engineering. He subsequently engaged in cognitive studies. Norman's combined interest in engineering and cognitive studies led him to an important insight. He came to realize that one of the reasons that our design environments did not function effectively was because they were designed on the basis of a combination of assumed human rationality, cost efficiency and aesthetics (Whitehead *et al.* 2018: 67). According to Norman, a key factor that was missing within the design and engineering sciences was a concern with how people actually behave. In a sense what Norman identified is a form of *Homo economicus* in the realms of the design sciences – a kind of *Homo engineericus* (someone who reads signs carefully, is able to remember complex instructions and always turns up to airports with plenty of time to navigate their way to their departure gate) (see Dyson & Sutherland 2021). The problem is that when you design worlds that assume the presence of *Homo engineericus* one can quickly make life more difficult to navigate for regular humans. This insight is essentially an extension of Herbert Simon's scissors, wherein not only does the environment not provide us with the necessary information we need to make good choices, but it deliberately obscures such knowledge on the basis of assumed wisdom. Listen to Norman's advice for the designers of early computer systems:

> System designers take note. Design the system for the person, not for the computer, not even for yourself. People are also information processing systems, with varying degrees of knowledge, varying degrees of experience. Remember, people's short-term memories are limited in size, and they learn and retrieve things best when there is a consistent reason for the name, the function, and the syntax. Friendly systems treat users as intelligent adults who, like normal adults, are forgetful, distracted, thinking of other things, and not quite as knowledgeable about the world as they themselves would like to be. (Norman 1981: 10)

Norman became particularly well known for his critique of early iterations of the Unix computer operating system (see Text Box 2.1). Within this critique he emphasized how poorly defined environments place too much stress on human cognition and contribute to user error. Norman's solution was to place human needs and limitations at the centre of design considerations. A central part of this approach to design was attempting to go with the grain of limited human cognition rather than just pretending that bounded rationality did not exist. A very simple example of this (which is a particular source of frustration for Norman) is the design of doors. If a door can only open and close in certain directions then make sure that you only have a handle on the side of the door you should pull, rather than also having a handle where there should be a push plate. Another key insight of Norman's work was a realization that if you wanted to foster more human-centred design then you should engage with people at every stage of the design process. Norman thus became a great advocate of participatory forms of design, within which people have a far greater say in the form that their design environments take.

Norman's insights (and the broader field of cognitive design) would ultimately influence far more than just the design of doors or even early computer operating systems. Norman supported the investigation into the 1979 Three Mile Island nuclear accident in Pennsylvania, United States. The user interface and design of control panel instruments at the nuclear plant were identified as contributory factors to the poor response to the accident (Walker 2004). Cognitive design would also play a crucial role in the development of nudging-type techniques. By suggesting that it was environments that could be targeted rather than people, cognitive design supported the more libertarian aspects of nudging. Norman's work was referenced in Thaler and Sunstein's 2008 book *Nudge* and he provided one of the endorsements on the book's cover.

BOX 2.1 DONALD NORMAN AND "THE TRUTH ABOUT UNIX"

In a paper published in *Datamation* in 1981 Donald Norman offered an insight into the contributions that cognitive design principles would make to the development of nudging.

Unix was an early computer operating system developed at Bell Telephone Laboratories, which have been at the forefront of some significant scientific breakthroughs, including the photovoltaic cell, the laser and the transistor. However, Norman's paper was not a celebration of Unix, it was an exploration of why "its user interface is horrid" (Norman 1981). A central aspect of Norman's interest in the failings of Unix stemmed from the fact that despite being a regular user of computer systems for 20 years as well as a design expert, he struggled to use Unix. Here we see Kahneman and Tversky's assertion that expertise is no protection to the cognitive limitations that characterize poor choice environments. Norman diagnosed the cognitive design failings of Unix on the following terms:

- It lacked *consistency* in its command functions: for example, the command for change password was "passwd", while the command for change working directory was "chdir". Notice here how the contraction of commands into shortened forms is not consistent: losing two letters in the password command seems hardly worth it, while there is no indication that it has anything to do with password change. While "chdir" combined two words that have already been contracted to their first two and three letters respectively, rendering its meaning opaque.
- It failed to provide regular *feedback* to users. Norman actually described this as a lack of "friendliness" built into the Unix system, which he described as taking on the personality of a "recluse, hidden from the user, silent in operation" (*ibid.*). According to Norman, Unix appeared to work on the principle of "no news is good news", but this resulted in users not knowing

the state of the system, when/if errors had been made, or even when one inadvertently left the system.

- Due to a lack of intuitive functions and feedback, the Unix system *placed pressure on the cognitive capabilities of the user* to remember what they needed and to be able to discern the needs of an otherwise silent system. While Norman does not formally reference the work of Herbert Simon, his solution to the problems of Unix reflect a sharpening of the contextual blade of Simon's scissors so as to take the strain off the cognitive blade. Norman argued that Unix should be more consistent in its use of commands and deploy mnemonic devices to make them easier to understand. He also claimed that the system should provide more regular feedback, which should support the construction of mental models that could help the users better understand how the system worked and what it needed. On these terms the emerging field of cognitive design can be seen as a field connected to the practical diagnosis and treatment of the problems of bounded rationality.

The take-up and take-off of nudging

From libertarian paternalism to nudging

So far, we have charted the ideas and practices that informed the development of something which eventually got called nudging. Nudging, however, actually started life under a different name: "libertarian paternalism" (or "soft paternalism"). At a meeting in 1997, a number of academics working at the interface of psychology and economics considered the application of behavioural economic ideas to public policy issues (see Lowenstein & Chater 2017: 26). A key goal of this meeting was not only to think of ways in which the now well-established insights of the behavioural and psychological sciences could be applied to public policy, but to also consider how they could take a form that would appeal across the political spectrum. In this context, the late 1990s mark the point at which political considerations enter the story of nudge. The thinking, we can only assume, would have been that ensuring that behavioural public policy appealed to both the right and left of politics would maximize its real-world impacts. If behavioural forms of public policy were seen as too left-wing and interventionist it is likely that they would have remained fairly marginal policy ideas. However, it is important to note that in the book *Against Autonomy* (2012), Sarah Conly argues that insights into cognitive biases and human behavioural shortcomings do not necessarily lead to libertarian paternalism. They could be used to support the development of more interventionist and coercive forms of government. Conly thus claims, "We need [...] a democratically elected government, but one in which the government is allowed to pass legislation that protects citizens from themselves, just as we allow legislation to protect us from others. I argue for the justifiability of coercive paternalism, for laws that force people to do what is good for them" (Conly 2012: 5).

We reflect on Conly here for two reasons. First, because she draws attention to what is at the very heart of the nudging movement and the debates that surround it: namely the question of if and how actors in the public and private sectors should *protect us from ourselves*. Second, because her suggestion of coercive paternalism (surely better to call it *democratic paternalism*) reveals a clear alternative application of the insights of the behavioural and psychological sciences to public policymaking than nudging.

If the 1997 meeting of behavioural scientists is when politics enters the history of nudging it is interesting to reflect on the precise nature of that politics. To put things another way, we are interested in how behavioural science could have entered the policy-making process if nudging had not been predominantly developed in the United States. The US political context clearly shaped a form of behavioural public policy that prioritized personal liberty and freedom much more than it may have done in Europe, for example. It is important thus to note that nudging is one potential response to the key question of if and how actors in the public and private sectors *should protect us from ourselves*. Although you do not see many references to nudging in China this is probably not because the behavioural sciences are not informing public policy interventions there, but because such interventions have not been framed by questions of personal liberty. It is thus important to recognize the different directions that nudging could have taken because nudging has both opened up new opportunities for psychology to influence policymaking and closed off other chances to apply behavioural insights to social problems (see Lowenstein & Chater 2017).

Following the 1997 meeting two papers were published in 2003 which together established the outline of what would become nudging. The first paper proposed the idea of "asymmetric paternalism" (see Camera *et al.*

2003). According to Camera *et al.*, "A regulation is asymmetrically paternalistic if it creates large benefits for those who make errors, while imposing little or no harm on those who are fully rational. Such regulations are relatively harmless to those who reliably make decisions in their best interest, while at the same time advantageous to those making suboptimal choices" (Camera *et al.* 2003: 1212).

Asymmetric paternalism argues for the need to address behavioural bias in the population but in such a way that is not burdensome to those who are less prone to such errors. The kind of interventions suggested by advocates of asymmetric paternalism are the same as many of those we now call nudges (such as the resetting of defaults). However, there are two features of asymmetric paternalism that mark it out as distinctive: (1) it is predicated upon the fact that there are those who are prone to behavioural biases and those that are more rational; and (2), related to this, asymmetrical paternalism seeks to preserve the freedom of more rational actors by making it easier for them to resist paternalist policies. The gentleness of asymmetric paternalism then is based not on a desire to preserve freedom for all, but to primarily protect the liberties of purportedly more rational segments of the population.

The second key paper of 2003 proposed a different form of paternalism: Thaler and Sunstein's libertarian paternalism (Thaler & Sunstein 2003). Libertarian paternalism is different to asymmetric paternalism more in purpose than form. Unlike asymmetric paternalism, it presumes that pretty much everyone is subject to behavioural biases. Following on from this assumption, it does not seek to place limits on paternalistic policy so as to protect fully rational actors from unnecessary interference, but instead seeks to ensure a degree of freedom for all. What asymmetrical and libertarian paternalism have in common is an assertion that rational forms of behaviour are a norm which policy should be used to correct towards, and that many social problems can be traced back to the decision-making blind spots that are generated by bounded rationality.

These papers on asymmetric and libertarian styles of paternalism would lay the foundation for what would become more popularly known as nudging. It is interesting to note that Thaler and Sunstein originally planned to call their book libertarian paternalism but were persuaded by their publishers to title it *Nudge*. The key features and principles of nudging, as expressed in Thaler and Sunstein's book, can be summarized as follows:

1. Not protecting people from their selves is not a neutral position: the world is already structured in ways which tend to make effective decision-making difficult and seeks to exploit human weakness to foster harmful social trends (i.e., the accumulation of debt, climate change, unhealthy eating practices, etc.).
2. Behavioural biases are a major source of social problems and should be acknowledged and addressed within public policy.
3. Behavioural biases are held by all people and cannot be overcome in any meaningful sense.
4. Behavioural biases can be used to help protect people from themselves.
5. By targeting people's choice architectures it is possible to utilize biases to change behaviour in a way that does not undermine personal liberty.
6. Personal liberty is preserved within paternalistic polices when people can easily resist related policies and are presented with behavioural choices.

Feature 1 of nudging is clearly indebted to Simon's long-established notion of bounded rationality. However, in Thaler and Sunstein's interpretation it is not just that people have cognitive limitations and that environments may not support effective decision-making. Nudging recognizes that commercial hands already wield Simon's scissors to meet their own ends. In this context, bounded rationality is no longer simply seen to be a natural feature of human biology or environmental materiality – it is an artificially enhanced and exploited feature of collective existence. The paternalism of nudging is thus predicated on an attempt to try and level the behavioural playing field and to give citizens a reasonable chance of protecting themselves from themselves.

Features 2 and 3 are clearly products of the work of Kahneman, Tversky and behavioural economists more generally. Feature 2 is particularly significant because it reveals the way in which nudging equates the identification of human behavioural flaws (not being able to plan for the future particularly well, disliking change, going with the social herd) with the production of certain social problems (the challenges of supporting an ageing population, inaction on climate change, and obesity). As we shall discuss at greater length in Chapter 4 the causal link made here between behavioural biases and social problems is problematic for at least two reasons. First, it unhelpfully equates complex social problems with personal behavioural flaws and thus fails to acknowledge the structural nature of many socio-economic and environmental problems (see Lowenstein & Chater 2017: 33). Second, it fails to appreciate the value of behavioural heuristics and biases in human decision-making. Nudging has thus become synonymous with correcting behavioural biases and of attempting to shift human behaviour back to rational economic expectations (Hallsworth & Kirkman 2020: 39). As we shall discuss later, this normative correction of human behaviours towards colder forms of economic logic has proven controversial, particularly when it has been associated with Thaler and Sunstein's advocacy of investment in the financial markets (Whitehead *et al.* 2018). Feature 3 is interesting because it reveals the particular way in which nudging mixes science with politics. The assertion that behavioural biases are largely unwanted but inescapable aspects of human existence is supported by the scientific inquiries of behavioural economists. Other psychological scientists, however, recognize both the potentially positive role biases can play in human behaviour and suggest a human ability to learn how to contextually adapt our heuristics so they can be used more effectively (Gigerenzer 2015). Interpreting behavioural biases as harmful and inevitable may have a scientific basis, but it also has certain political advantages. If biases are irrevocable, it is surely best to change the context of behaviour (the choice architecture) rather than the individual (Feature 5). This is therefore a scientific perspective that is well aligned with Thaler and Sunstein's desire to ensure that nudging is likely to be accepted within more libertarian political cultures.

A focus on transforming choice environments rather than people is precisely why cognitive design and engineering was so important within the development of nudging. Cognitive design and engineering essentially offered a specialist field that revealed the way in which virtual and real-world environments could be shaped in ways that promoted certain forms of behaviour and inhibited others. Implicit within nudgers' use of cognitive design insights is the realization that cognitive biases not only reflect behavioural pathologies but also offer a vector for behavioural correction (see Feature 4 above). Nudgers, for example, often talk about the way in which the design of supermarkets promotes unhealthy eating behaviours. The placement of sweets and chocolate bars in the lanes where people queue to pay for their shopping is clearly an attempt to tempt shoppers (and in particular children) into purchasing sugary snacks (such tactics have been referred to as "dark nudges"; Petticrew *et al.* 2020). The response of nudgers and cognitive designers has been to promote the redesign of supermarkets in order to promote healthier behaviours. For example, the establishment of alcohol only check-outs in supermarkets in Scotland has been proposed to de-normalize alcohol consumption and to mobilize peer pressure (as those buying alcohol could be more clearly seen by other shoppers) to reduce consumption (BBC 2016).

Feature 5 of nudging (that they are easy to resist and preserve choice) is central to its identity as a gentle form of power. The libertarian credentials of nudging rest, in part, on the fact that they do not seek to generate long-term changes in the values held by people, but merely reshape the choice environments within which they operate. In this context, the preservation of choice is a particularly important feature of nudging. So, the use of alcohol-only check-outs attempts to mobilize peer pressure to reduce the social ease of buying alcohol (when hidden amongst other groceries). However, such an intervention still preserves the element of choice.

Policy take-off: from nudge units to nudging ecosystems

The five key features of nudging outlined above reflect the translation of a particular strand of the behavioural and psychological sciences, filtered through the design sciences, into a politically acceptable policy tool. It is not the only way in which behavioural psychology or behavioural economics can, or has, influenced public policy, but it is arguably the most significant. The particular combination of libertarianism and paternalism that Thaler and Sunstein baked into nudging was designed to ensure that related policies would have wide political appeal. On the evidence of the rapid take-up and ultimate take-off of nudging in the second decade of the twenty-first century, you would have to conclude that Thaler and Sunstein were successful in their designs. The UK government had shown interest in the application of the behavioural sciences to public policy for a number of years (see Jones *et al.* 2013). However, following his election as prime minister in 2010 David Cameron sought to make nudging a defining tool of his administration. Richard Thaler had advised Cameron's Conservative Party in the run up the 2010 election and would play a role in the formation of the first dedicated national nudge unit in the UK later that year (Hallsworth &

Kirkman 2020: 55). It was called the Behavioural Insights Team although it was inevitably referred to as "the nudge unit".

There are some features of the Behavioural Insights Team (BIT) that are worth reflecting on as they speak to the challenges that nudging experienced in its early take-up phase. While initially housed in the UK government's Cabinet Office, the BIT was designed as a sort of skunkworks operation, with a relatively high level of operational autonomy. This autonomy perhaps reflected the fact that many of the assumptions that informed the work of the nudge unit were too out of channel to be able to easily take seed within pre-existing government institutions. Once established, the BIT did two things fairly quickly. First, it emphasized the importance of coupling the application of nudge-style policies with randomized control trials (RCTs) (Hallsworth & Kirkman 2020: 58–9). RCTs required that the impacts of nudging policy interventions were measured in relation to control groups that were not subjected to the nudges. RCTs were seen as an important way of proving the effectiveness of nudges and of helping to establish their credentials within a sceptical policy community (see Jones & Whitehead 2018). Second, the BIT was quick to ensure that they were not too narrowly associated with nudges (see Halpern 2016). While nudges were deployed and tested by the BIT, the team were keen to avoid the controversies that rapidly became associated with nudging and to explore broader applications of the behavioural sciences within public policy (a field that is now often referred to as "behavioural public policy").

On the other side of the Atlantic nudging found an even more direct route into public policy. Following his election as president in 2008, Barack Obama appointed his friend, and the co-author of *Nudge*, Cass Sunstein to be the head of the Office of Information and Regulatory Affairs. In this position Sunstein was responsible for the assessment, verification and design of government regulations of every kind. In his 2013 book *Simpler: The Future of Government* Sunstein recounts his time as nudger-in-chief and his attempts to integrate the principles of nudging into federal regulations. It is interesting to note that during his time in government Sunstein was critiqued from the right as being too paternalistic and from the progressive left as being anti-regulation. During Obama's second presidential term, and following the departure of Sunstein, the federal government established the Social and Behavioural Sciences Team (lead by Maya Shankar) to integrate the behavioural and psychological sciences more directly into all aspects of government activities. This was followed in 2015 by an executive order – a directive by the president – entitled "Using behavioural science to better serve the America people". Although the Social and Behavioural Science Team did not survive within the Trump administration (we guess there is a limit to how much political future-proofing any policy approach can be given) its work continued in other branches of the government.

Although the UK and USA were significant government centres for the initial policy uptake of nudging, countries including Canada, Germany, the Netherlands, Lebanon and France were also relatively early adopters. Following its early take-up in certain countries nudging went through a rapid take-off phase when it became a policy technique in vogue (see Figure 2.2 above). By 2014 it was estimated that 51 countries around the world were deploying some form of nudging programme at a national level (Whitehead *et al.* 2014). The globalization of nudge was in part based on the example set by early adopter countries, with the UK's BIT acting as a prominent international consultant (Whitehead 2019). But the international spread of nudging was also facilitated by prominent international organizations such as the United Nations, World Bank, OECD and European Union. During the take-off phase of nudging these organizations all produced reports that explored the potential application of nudging in a diverse range of policy areas. The global spread of nudging created what Hallsworth and Kirkman have described as a "behavioural insights ecosystem" within which numerous public bodies and political institutions were involved in a collective public policy experiment to explore the potential of nudge-type policies (2020: 65–9). Over time, this ecosystem of nudging was expanded by the development of private-sector nudging consultancies such as Ogilvy Change and The Behavioural Architects. According to Hallsworth and Kirkman the formation of this nudging ecosystem reflected a "technocratic drive to improve how government works" (Hallsworth & Kirkman 2020: 63). This notion of pragmatic government became a defining characteristic of the global nudging ecosystem. As we have outlined above, however, the depiction of nudging as pragmatic obscures the inherent politics of nudging that was baked into its form and function during its inception. As we have also seen, the history of nudging is a complex mix of science, politics, biography and happenstance. The nature of this history serves to remind us of the different forms that nudging and broader forms of behavioural government could and may take in the future.

3

Nudges in practice

Armed with our knowledge of the emergence and development of nudging as a set of concepts and principles deployed by governments, corporations and designers, it is time to turn our attention to the practical application of nudging in different geographical and sectoral contexts. Geographically, the spread of nudging has been impressive. According to an OECD (2017) report, behavioural insights are being applied within public policy in over 200 public bodies throughout the world. The sectoral spread of the use of behavioural insights has been equally impressive. From relatively humble beginnings, behavioural and psychological insights are now being used to influence policy development and delivery in relation to a wide variety of policy sectors, including pro-environmental behaviours, energy use, economic behaviour, voting and minority language promotion. There is no clearer indication of the current significance of nudging than the fact that it has become over a few short years since the publication of Thaler and Sunstein's 2008 book, a mainstay of the political and popular lexicon. Although the specific details might remain abstruse, few are now unaware of the broad meaning of nudging in policy contexts.

Such a proliferation of nudging begs a series of questions, and it is these that we shall seek to answer in this chapter. First, what explains the widespread appeal of nudging? Why has it become such a popular approach to addressing different kinds of problematic behaviour? Why now? Or, in other words, what have been the specific conditions that explain the remarkable uptake of nudging principles and practices from 2008 onwards? We discuss how the current appeal of nudging derives largely from its ability to act as a relatively low-cost, technocratic and, allegedly, politically neutral way of enabling organizations, including the state, to grapple with a series of modern-day challenges.

Second, what forms have contemporary examples of nudging taken in different geographical and sectoral contexts? Even though behavioural insights are now being employed across the world, are they more popular in certain jurisdictions than others? Is nudging more popular in particular policy sectors than others? Is nudging more effective as a way of addressing certain policy ills than others? And, does nudging mean the same thing in these various geographical and sectoral contexts? Despite the claim that nudging now exists as part of a behavioural insights ecosystem that has spread throughout the world, our contention is that this is very much a variegated ecosystem, characterized by nuance and texture. We also claim that it is important to be aware of these distinctions and differences in the way in which nudging is being applied in practice.

The (widespread) appeal of nudging

What, therefore, explains the widespread appeal of nudging? And why has nudging become such a prevalent and popular way of addressing various policy ills in recent years? We outline a number of different potential explanations in the following discussion. Not one factor in isolation can explain the growing popularity of nudging. Rather they should be viewed as factors that have contributed, together, to a more active engagement with nudging.

Most accounts of nudging point to the growing influence of new understandings of behaviour on the formulation of public policy from the turn of the new millennium onwards (Halpern 2015). Key proponents of the insights of behavioural economics and the behavioural sciences were invited to speak to groups of policymakers and civil servants from a variety of countries during this period (Jones *et al.* 2013b). But thist does not explain why such interactions were becoming increasingly significant during this period. Patently, it was not because of the emergence of new academic knowledge at this time. As we showed in Chapter 2, the principles of behavioural economics and behavioural psychology had been discussed since the 1950s. Admittedly, certain new insights began to emerge during the new millennium, most notably in relation to neuroscience, and it is possible that these might have provided an additional impetus to the policy engagement with nudging. Nikolas Rose (2010), for example, has suggested that the emergence of a so-called "neuromolecular gaze" in the new millennium has energized debates about the potential of "screening and intervening" or, in other words, using neuroscience as a way of identifying future problematic behaviours and correcting for them prior to them happening. Despite the significance of such developments, it is unlikely that the growing appetite for using behavioural insights as a way of informing a new approach to public policy can be ascribed solely to the supply of new academic insights from neuroscience.

More promising lines of enquiry, we would argue, derive from an exploration of the *demand* from governments and public-sector institutions for new approaches to address various social and environmental ills. First, we claim that the growing appetite for a behaviourally informed public policy at the turn of the new millennium stemmed from a growing realization that neoliberalism as a political and economic agenda had led to increasing levels of personal debt and financial mismanagement, the rise of new forms of personal health problems (particularly obesity), perceived problems of social disorder and family breakdown, as well as a series of challenges linked to climate change. All of these have generated debate concerning the role of state institutions in redressing the harmful socio-economic and environmental practices associated with the many "indulgences" of a neoliberal society (Head 2022). And yet, this was a state for which widespread and far-reaching intervention or regulation was anathema. As a result, nudging offered an attractive "third way" for the state. Nudging preserved the assumption that freedom to pursue economic self-interest was an efficient and effective way of organizing a social economy. However, nudging introduced an important caveat, namely that people do not always recognize what is in their own best interests (due to short-term temptation, error, inertia and other psychological traits) (Jones *et al*. 2013a). Nudges were deemed to be an effective way of circumventing that conundrum by preserving choice while, at the same time, subtly framing decisions so that "better" choices were made by more people on a more regular basis.

Second, it has been suggested that the growing appetite for nudging policies derived from the fact that they were – and continue to be – perceived as relatively cheap means of addressing various social and environmental ills. For financially-constrained states, like the UK during the period of austerity beginning 2008 (and which has arguably not left us ever since), nudging represented a much cheaper way of addressing policy ills than more conventional forms of regulation. Citizens and consumers could be subtly cajoled into making better decisions by clever choice architects, rather than being penalized for making poor decisions through legal enforcement measures. It was such a line of thinking that led to experiments in "no frills" forms of government during this period (see Text Box 3.1).

BOX 3.1 BARNET COUNCIL, A CONSERVATIVE OUTRIDER FOR NO-FRILLS GOVERNMENT

The Conservative-led Barnet Council in north London sought to use nudging as a means of reducing council costs from 2009 onwards. Following the example of "no-frills" or "budget" airlines, such as Easyjet or Ryanair, the aim of the council, outlined by its then leader, Mike Freer, was to "target our interventions" rather than reduce the extent of the services the council provided. Freer elaborated that "some things will be cheap and cheerful and in other areas we will provide complete services". New policies demonstrated an ideological commitment to the principles of behaviour change, for example, attempts were made to reduce the carbon footprint of the residents of Finchley. Residents were encouraged to make face-to-face commitments with council canvassers to cut their energy use and were encouraged to follow the example of their neighbours, whose participation in the scheme was advertised on surrounding lampposts – using the nudge tactics of harnessing commitment and shaping social norms. It is clear that Barnet Council during this period was viewed as a radical outrider of a more Conservative vision for nudging, in which behaviour change policies were seen as significant ways of liberalizing public services and reducing the "big" state to more intelligent and allegedly cheaper little nudges.

Such developments, as outlined in the case study box above, highlight the appeal of nudging. It represents – at least at face value – a cheap and efficient form of state intervention. Of course, what such claims fail to acknowledge are the additional costs associated with delivering effective forms of nudging, not least in association with the evaluation of nudging interventions, for instance in relation to randomized controlled trials (Jones & Whitehead 2018). David Halpern and Michael Sanders (2016: 53) claim that "[a]lthough detailed cost–benefit analyses are not yet available, we estimate that behaviorally inspired interventions can help government agencies save hundreds of millions of dollars per year". There is a need to test the veracity of this claim, but this is itself a difficult task due to the need to isolate the costs and savings arising from nudging interventions. What is more important, arguably, is the fact that there has been a widespread *belief* for the past 20 or so years among public servants that nudging is cheaper than regulations, laws and stricter forms of policy intervention.

A third contributory factor that explains the growing significance of nudging at the turn of the millennium was its widespread political appeal and, seemingly, non-ideological nature. As suggested earlier, nudging represented a practical way of applying a "third-way" approach to politics and public policy (Jones *et al.* 2013a). The pragmatism of nudging is especially appealing in the US, where the partisan nature of politics can hamper attempts to achieve policy goals. For Johnson (2016: no page), "in an age of congressional gridlock and partisan bickering, [nudging] offers a glimmer of hope that government can do a little something that's uncontroversial and positive. When aspirations for hope and change are disappointed, technocratic fixes will do". Nudging, in this sense, is viewed as the archetypal example of "what works government" or, in other words, a wholly pragmatic approach to policymaking, which is allegedly devoid of any ideological basis. And of course, the political malleability of nudging is further illustrated by the various critiques of nudging offered by those on different extremes of the political spectrum. For liberals and conservatives, there is a belief that nudging represents an unwanted interference by the state in our everyday lives. For those advocating more interventionist approaches to government, nudging has been criticized for being a tentative and half-hearted means of addressing far-reaching social, economic and environmental ills. As a result, nudging, as Table 3.1 shows, is an approach to policy-making that is supported and criticized, in equal measure, from all directions!

These three sets of reasons for the emergence of nudging as a new approach to public policy are important in their own right but they also point to the need to consider a series of implications for the current implementation of nudging policies. These implications, we argue, encourage us to think about a nudging ecosystem that is highly varied in character.

First, we should appreciate that while nudging represents a popular approach to addressing various policy ills, its use is highly contingent. In broad terms, nudging is used to target problematic behaviours that are deemed to be unsuitable to more regulatory interventions (for political or more practical reasons). And yet, when one makes such a statement, one is

Table 3.1 The contradictory appeal of, and distrust towards, nudging

	Advocates of nudging	Critics of nudging
Liberal/conservatives	Nudging represents a way of minimizing the size of the state, preserving choice, while still enabling one to grapple with wicked problems	Nudging represents an unwarranted and paternalistic intrusion by a "nanny state" into everyday freedoms
Interventionists	Nudging represents an effective way of intervening in challenging issues created by neoliberalism. It is politically palatable to a public that is suspicious of widespread state intervention	Nudging is merely a way of tinkering with widespread structural problems and there is a need for more fundamental policy interventions to address multiple wicked problems
Libertarian paternalists	Nudging represents an ideal trade-off between intervening in human behaviour and maintenance of choice	Nudging represents the worst of both worlds in that it represents a manipulation of individuals while maintaining an illusion of choice

forced to recognize that what are deemed to be problematic behaviours, and what is deemed to be a suitable target for nudge-like interventions, vary over time and space. For instance, our previous research has shown the state's appetite for nudging in relation to a series of problematic health behaviours, whether in the context of obesity, smoking and sexual health (Pykett *et al.* 2016). The adoption of such health nudges followed a period during which states across the world had adopted a more neoliberal approach to the same problematic behaviours, with individuals being free to practise unhealthy lifestyles as long as they did not harm others. However, the recent Covid-19 pandemic was characterized by the most stringent controls on personal freedoms in relation to health witnessed for decades, with individuals in the majority of countries confined to their homes for long periods of time. While the public health threat posed by the pandemic may have justified such drastic interventions, it illustrates the way in which different policy approaches – some more interventionist, some more neoliberal and some based on nudging – become more or less acceptable at different points in time. Similar variations may well be witnessed in more spatial contexts (e.g. Sunstein *et al.* 2017).

Second, even though nudging is being employed in different places, it might mean something different, or be conceptualized in different ways, in different places. For instance, nudging is viewed in the US as either a non-partisan and technocratic approach to public policy (by its proponents) and as a mark of a manipulative and over-reaching state (by its detractors). In some Nordic countries, where the interventionist nature of social dem-ocratic states is more accepted, nudging is viewed as a frivolous and largely unnecessary approach to public policy. In the UK for much of the twenty-first century, it has been viewed as an appropriate policy tool, especially given that it is seen as something that is reflective of a more consensual approach to politics. While nudging has been used to inform public policy in different states across the world, there is also potential for its application to vary from one state to another as ideas become meshed with the political cultures that exist in different countries. As we argued earlier in this volume, it is import-ant to realize there may well be multiple versions of nudging in existence in different states, in different policy sectors and at different times. To speak of one approach to nudging, therefore, may well be misleading. Although we speak of nudging in the singular in this book, it is worth remembering that nudging is likely to mean slightly different things in different policy, sectoral and geographical settings.

Third, and following on from the previous point, any simple policy trans-fer of nudging: geographically, across policy sectors, from private to public sector, and so on, may be unwise. The contexts within which nudging is applied vary so a process of *translation* is needed from one deployment to another. Rather than merely noting the similarities between nudging poli-cies adopted in different jurisdictions and assuming that some form of policy transfer has taken place between them, researchers have increasingly sought to explain how such policy similarities have come into being. We need to be sensitive to the way in which policymakers in new jurisdictions make sense of policy initiatives elsewhere, and the need for an ongoing process of policy translation. A key aspect of policy translation is the degree to which policy ideas such as nudging become accepted by politicians, civil servants, policy implementers, and the general public as ones that are consonant with their worldviews. The successful translation of a nudging policy involves, there-fore, the social and spatial embedding of a policy into a cultural context so that it gains widespread currency as a means of tackling a particular social, economic, or environmental ill within a particular place.

The various applications of nudge

Given this broad context, it is time to provide some examples of the various ways in which nudge policies and interventions have been applied within this variegated ecosystem. Of necessity, we cannot provide a fully comprehensive account of the various contexts within which nudging has been used as a policy tool (see John *et al.* 2013; Pykett *et al.* 2016; Whitehead *et al.* 2018). Rather, we seek to provide illustrative examples of different contexts within which nudging has been applied, focusing specifically on examples that demonstrate the value of nudging as a means of addressing different kinds of individual and public benefit and harm.

When and when not to nudge?

There are two main ways of assessing the appropriateness or otherwise of policy approaches informed by nudging. First, and following on from the discussion in the previous section, numerous authors have questioned the ethics of nudging. Are there certain situations in which it is either more or less ethical to employ nudging as a technique of government? Are there certain situations in which the charges of manipulation levelled towards nudging are more acceptable than others? This is a theme to which we return in Chapter 4.

A second consideration concerns which policy contexts are likely to lead to the most effective application of nudging as a governmental tool? Thaler (2016: 50) provides a useful guide when he observes: "[p]sychologists tell us that in order to learn from experience, two ingredients are necessary: frequent practice and immediate feedback". The quality of our decision-making in contexts where those decisions are infrequent and provide little or delayed feedback is, therefore, more likely to be compromised, with nudging being viewed as a potential aid to making better decisions. Named in honour of another academic with whom he was in debate around this issue, Thaler has devised the so-called Binmore continuum, which further emphasizes the significance of nudging as a tool with which to target infrequent choices and/or ones with little or no opportunity for feedback:

> On the left I started with cafeteria lunch (daily), then milk and bread (twice a week), and so forth up to sweaters, cars, and homes,

career choices, and spouses (not more than two or three per lifetime for most of us). Notice the trend. We do small stuff often enough to learn to get it right, but when it comes to choosing a home, a mortgage, or a job, we don't get much practice or opportunities to learn. And when it comes to saving for retirement, barring reincarnation we do that exactly once.   (Thaler 2016: 50)

The Binmore continuum, while useful, can be criticized when it is used to determine the appropriateness of using nudging as a policy tool. The continuum accurately represents situations in which individuals are more likely to make better or worse decisions. In general, we make more informed and better decisions when those are done regularly, with immediate feedback provided. However, this does not mean that nudging ought to be viewed as a necessarily appropriate response to infrequent decisions. There are many different ways of responding to such scenarios, including the provision of better information for those making decisions or making poor decisions more expensive; neither of which would represent nudging per se. Nonetheless, the Binmore continuum has been used to provide some indication of the contexts in which nudging could or should be used as a way of aiding decision-making.

Nudging mechanisms

Another way of categorizing nudging in practice is in relation to the mechanisms used to encourage individuals and groups to act in particular ways. In broad terms, we argue that it is possible to identify four types of mechanisms linked to nudging (Jones *et al.* 2013a): (1) spatial design and choice architecture; (2) temporal ordering; (3) measures to rationalize the brain; and (4) the promotion of social norms. First, certain forms of nudging use choice architectures to orient people towards particular behaviours. At one level, a focus on choice architectures highlights the pernicious temptations that are etched into the environments we encounter on an everyday basis, such as the temptations associated with "ambient gambling" opportunities in pubs, cafes and taxicab offices (Welsh *et al.* 2014). However, the restructuring of choice architectures can be used to facilitate positive behavioural outcomes. Examples would include the redesigning of stairwells to encourage people to exercise more at work, to the more wholesale planning of streets so as to promote community safety and enhanced opportunities for social interaction (see Jones *et al.* 2013a for an analysis of DIY streets).

A second type of nudging emphasizes the need to manipulate time in relation to decisions and behaviours. Attempts to promote more pro-environmental behaviours in the UK, for example, have examined the potential of using temporal windows of opportunity to promote lifestyle changes at opportune moments – both in terms of moments of political acceptability and important life stages or events (e.g. DEFRA 2007: 22). For example, a good time to promote the fitting of loft insulation is at the moment someone moves in to a house, as the loft is most likely empty. Similarly, there has been considerable debate with regard to the need to develop new policies on gambling, which seek to help problem gamblers make themselves subject to self-imposed bans from casinos and other gambling establishments. The significance of such schemes is that they seek to circumvent a temporal tension between a rational decision made by a problem gambler in their more lucid moments and the irrational decisions made by the same individuals in the "heat of the moment" (Welsh *et al.* 2014).

A third group of nudging mechanisms aim to work through and overcome the "predictable irrationality" (Ariely 2009) of human behaviour to promote choices which we would make if our brains worked in a consistently rational manner. The administrative mechanism of default pensions is one example. The use of "automatic enrolment" in pension schemes, while introducing a presumption for individuals to save, retains the opportunity to opt out. This kind of policy recognizes systematic behavioural flaws such as inertia and a sense of powerlessness in the face of the complexity of the decisions involved (see Chapter 4 for a critical analysis of the application of nudging to pension savings). Nudging also aims to overcome systematic mistakes in human decision-making through assisting our automatic minds to make more reflexive decisions. The use of drinks calculators in alcohol harm reduction strategies, for example, aim to communicate risk more effectively, with the hope of enabling individuals to make informed decisions.

A final group of nudges are associated with the promotion of particular social norms. By using marketing and communications technologies, attempts have been made to change behavioural cultures. For example, the Act on CO_2 campaign website in the UK provides social networking opportunities such as the "People Power Challenge", involving people in

Portsmouth, Newcastle and Birmingham in a competition to cut their CO_2 emissions (Pykett *et al.* 2016). This encourages identification with particular towns and a sense of regional pride in pro-environmental behaviours. Such initiatives are part of a wider mobilization by government of significant intermediaries – teachers, parents, children, friends, youth workers, community activists, celebrities, and so on – in order to change behaviour indirectly through leadership, peer-to-peer support and advice, and norm setting. This reflects a shift in approach from advice coming from on high to being something that is shared from peer to peer.

Nudging: benefit and harm

A final way of categorizing nudging relates to the kind of benefit and/or harm related to different kinds of behaviour. Historically, the liberal philosophy of government has determined that state intervention in the regulation of personal conduct is only legitimate if it serves to prevent harm to others (Mill 1859). Nudging has circumvented traditional, liberal modes of limitation on state action and has opened up new registers of legitimate governmental activity, with attempts being made to address harm or potential harms, among other things, to the self, to other individuals, to society at large and to the environment (see Table 3.2).

First, let us address those instances of nudging that centre on reducing harm to the self. This is perhaps the most novel aspect of the recent turn to nudging as a policy tool. As noted above, there has been a reticence

Table 3.2 Nudging as an attempt to mitigate different types of harm and promote different benefits

Types of harm/benefit	Example
Of harm/benefit to oneself	Attempts to reduce over-consumption, e.g. of alcohol, processed food, salt
Of harm/benefit to other individuals	Attempts to encourage altruistic behaviour, e.g. organ donation, charitable giving
Of harm/benefit to the state or society at large	Attempts to make individuals productive members of society, e.g. saving for a pension, obtaining employment, promptly paying taxes
Of harm/benefit to the environment	Attempts to encourage pro-environmental behaviours, e.g. recycling, using public transport

within public policy informed by liberal ideals to interfere in behaviours that merely cause harm to the self. Increasingly, however, nudging has been used as a way of tackling the over-indulgences associated with neoliberalism and, particularly, those over-indulgences that are deemed to cause harm to the self. In this respect, nudging can be viewed as something that seeks to alleviate the multiple neuroses said to affect citizens in the contemporary world (Isin 2004). However, nudging diverges from more therapeutic attempts to address the neurotic citizen by bypassing entirely the irrational mind – explicitly attempting to take neurosis and anxiety out of the equation. Instead of targeting neuroses or encouraging individuals to improve themselves through their own education and effort, nudging targets a type of citizen-fool, seeking to prevent "forever-flawed", irrational humans making things worse for themselves. There are numerous examples of policies and interventions that seek to nudge flawed individuals into better decisions, which can improve their health, wealth and happiness (see example in Text Box 3.2).

BOX 3.2 REDUCING SALT CONSUMPTION IN ARGENTINA

A notable recent example of nudging to prevent harm to self can be seen in attempts made in Argentina to reduce the daily salt intake of its citizens. Prior to starting its new policy interventions in 2011, daily consumption of salt in the country was high, with the average Argentinian consuming 13g of salt every day, which is between twice and three times the recommended amount. Resulting levels of hypertension or high blood pressure among the population were also problematic. As a result of the perceived inability of Argentinians to self-regulate their own consumption of salt, the government has undertaken a multi-pronged approach (Allemandi et al. 2015). It has worked closely with food producers to reduce the amount of salt added to dough. A small-scale and localized agreement with the bakers of bread in March 2012 expanded into a more widespread and national voluntary agreement with the producers of processed food in September of the same year, with international companies, such as Nestle and Kraft Foods, signing up. This agreement formed a cornerstone of the so-called "Menos Sal, Mas Vida" (Less Salt, More Life) initiative. More importantly in the context of our discussion, there have been efforts to nudge individuals to consume less salt. In a widely-reported experiment, saltshakers were removed from tables in restaurants in Buenos Aries. Saltshakers were still available for customers, but they were encouraged to taste their food before asking for additional salt. The aim of this experiment was to counter the almost subconscious and unthinking tendency for many individuals in restaurants to add salt to their food without tasting it. In addition, it has arguably created somewhat of a stigma associated with adding salt to one's food, since customers have to explicitly request a saltshaker. Customers' responses to this nudge have been varied, perhaps betraying the tendency of nudging to polarize opinions. Some customers recognized the value of the nudge in helpfully creating a new norm in which the addition of salt was viewed as unnecessary. Others viewed the new nudging approach as a "prohibition" on their rights, calling instead for better education of individuals concerning the perils associated with a diet high in salt. Whatever the ethics associated with this approach, there is some evidence to suggest that it has been effective. It has been reported that the average daily consumption of salt in Argentina fell by 18 per cent between 2011 and 2015 (IFPRI 2016: 51).

A second set of nudging policies focus on reducing the harm (or, alternatively, increasing the benefit) that one individual might do to another person as a result of their decisions. Of course, reducing interpersonal harm has been a mainstay of more traditional forms of public policy, witnessed most clearly in the context of various penal laws. But it is significant that the insights of nudging can be harnessed to reduce harm and, more importantly, maximize the benefit that might arise for other individuals. Nudging, in this latter context, has been employed as a technique to encourage charitable donations, with Indranil Goswami and Oleg Urminsky (2016: 829) claiming that "[c]ontrary to the view that setting defaults will backfire, defaults increased revenue". However, it is in the context of organ donation that the debates around inter-personal benefits of nudging have been at their most prevalent. Thaler and Sunstein (2008) claim that the use of mandated choice can act as a useful tool to encourage higher levels of organ donation or, in other words, an approach in which people are required by law to state whether they are willing or not to donate their organs following their deaths. Adopting this approach, it is argued, bypasses the tendency of individuals to be reticent to think about their own long-term future, particularly a future in which they are dead. Others have argued in favour of an alternative default position in which it is presumed that an individual is willing to donate their organs unless they have specified otherwise. This has been the policy in Wales, where both the authors of this book live and work, since 2015 (Whitehead *et al.* 2018: 81–2). However, the debate is still ongoing about the relative effectiveness of such approaches (see Chapter 4 for a critical analysis of nudging in organ donation programmes).

What is most significant about such policies is that nudging is used to address behaviours that cause very little harm or benefit to the individual concerned. After all, the individual will be dead at the time during which their organs will be harvested. Rather, organ donation revolves around managing harm and especially benefit to other individuals. At one level, the act of donation can lead to harm to the family and friends of the deceased. However, organ donation is clearly and predominantly an act that maximizes the benefits accruing to other individuals, namely organ recipients. The donor is, largely, absent from these calculations concerning relative harm and benefit to other individuals. How, therefore, might one engage the individual donor more effectively, particularly in relation to potential benefits arising from donating one's organs? Admittedly, public campaigns to promote organ donation have conventionally focused on the positive emotional benefits that can arise for the donor as a result of giving the "gift of life" (Morgan & Miller 2002). However, a new kind of approach has been adopted in Israel since 2008; one that has explicitly attempted to create a direct benefit to individuals who choose to donate their organs (see Text Box 3.3).

BOX 3.3 RECONFIGURING NOTIONS OF HARM AND BENEFIT IN RELATION TO ORGAN DONATION IN ISRAEL

Historically, rates of organ donation in Israel have been very low, with much of this reticence to donate related to a belief that organ donation is prohibited under Jewish law. In order to address this behavioural challenge, the Israeli state has created a new approach to organ donation. Since 2008, if two patients have the same medical need, priority will go to the patient who has signed an organ donor card, or whose family members have donated an organ; a policy that has been described popularly as "don't give, don't get". There are complex debates here, of course, around the assessment of relative medical need and about how often situations arise in which the medical needs of two individuals are exactly the same, thus leading to the new organ donation policy kicking in. However, there is some evidence to show that it has had a positive impact on rates of organ donation in Israel (Zaltzman 2018). And it is an impact that derives from an attempt to nudge individuals into thinking proactively about the benefits arising from organ donation for themselves, rather than for others. In the potential denial of significant benefits this policy stretches the notion of what may count as a nudge, but in its preservation of choice and the promotion of new social norms it does exhibit nudge-like qualities.

A third set of considerations about relative harm and benefit arise in the context of the impact of individuals on society or the state. It has been argued that the majority of research into behavioural insights has been characterized by a focus on individualized notions of behaviour and decision-making (Loewenstein & Chater 2017: 32–3). And yet, as we discussed above, there has been a growing appetite to examine the influence that social and cultural norms have on human decision-making. More broadly, even when policies informed by nudging target individual behaviour, we contend that there is an implicit recognition of the harm that the individual is causing society in general. For instance, even if interventions in Argentina in recent years have sought to reduce the level of salt consumption – primarily as a way of improving the health of the individuals concerned – there is still a secondary concern with the harm that this unchecked salt consumption causes society, the state and the economy (through additional pressures on healthcare systems, working days lost to ill health and so on). Certain authors maintain that nudging often includes such a sociological perspective: namely a concern with a potential harm to the self being implicitly associated with a similar concern about the harm of certain behaviours on society more broadly (Chriss 2015) (see Text Box 3.4).

BOX 3.4 EFFORTS TO REDUCE LEVELS OF UNEMPLOYMENT IN THE UK

In 2012 in the unassuming location of the Job Centre Plus offices in Loughton, Essex, a new strategy for getting people back to work was trialled. The trial involved splitting up 2,000 jobseekers into two randomized groups. The first of these two groups continued to follow the established Job Centre procedures, while the second were subjected to a new system. The new procedure involved a three-step process. The first step ensured that jobseekers actively talked to an official about seeking employment during their first visit to the Job Centre (previously this conversation was often delayed by up to two weeks). The second step used a series of "commitment devices", which established what the client would do over the coming two weeks to seek employment. The third step saw those clients who were still searching for work after eight weeks "building their psychological resilience and wellbeing" through "expressive writing and strengths identification" processes. The results of this trial saw those jobseekers in the "treatment groups" being 15–20 per cent more likely than those in the "control group" to be off benefits 13 weeks after visiting the Job Centre. It is significant that many of the lessons learnt from the trial location of Loughton have been promoted as more generic solutions to the problem of unemployment. A report by the Behavioural Insights Team (Briscese & Tan 2018: 5) emphasized the need to put behavioural solutions "that place people and their decision-making at the heart of the system" to help unemployed individuals find work. Some of the key lessons for designing employment systems for the unemployed include concentrating on relationship building (between the jobseeker and the relevant coach), simplifying communications to improve jobseekers' job search behaviour, and giving tailored assistance to jobseekers (*ibid.*: 6). Detail notwithstanding, what we witness here is the attempt to use behavioural insights to address unhelpful behaviours, which have a detrimental effect on both the individual concerned and society at large.

A fourth and final set of nudges focuses on addressing the harm that certain behaviours cause the environment. Arguably, the promotion of pro-environmental behaviours is more challenging than addressing other kinds of behaviour given that the notion of harm and benefit is often far removed from the individual concerned. In economic terms, the environment is an externality. The benefit to the individual arising from adopting pro-environmental behaviours is not always immediately evident, either in terms of its temporal or spatial impact. Similarly, the harm arising from behaviours that are destructive to the environment are not always evident to the individual concerned. To take the example of climate change, driving a car that produces high levels of carbon dioxide in the global north is more likely to contribute to a climate change that will have a negative effect on individuals, communities and environments in the global south. Such a spatial and temporal dislocation feeds into the effectiveness or otherwise of public campaigns to promote pro-environmental behaviours. Rachel Howell (2011) has shown that campaigns that feature desperate polar bears on disappearing ice flows do not have the hoped-for impact, precisely because they portray climate change in a way that is divorced geographically and biologically from the humans whose actions are contributing to climate change in the first place. How, therefore, can one seek to change environmental behaviours for the better and what is the role of nudging in all of this?

Fredrik Carlsson *et al.* (2021) review the potential positive impact of so-called green nudges in various contexts. Some "pure green nudges" seek to bypass human consciousness to a large degree, with notions of relative harm and benefit to the environment being addressed solely by the choice-architects that manipulate the decisions made by unsuspecting citizens and consumers. The effectiveness of these pure green nudges is mixed. Pro-environmental energy choices in Germany were higher in situations in which the pro-environmental choice was the default. Conversely, providing information about the lifetime energy costs of electrical goods did not encourage consumers to buy the most energy efficient products. Carlsson *et al.* (2021: 218) discuss another type of green nudge that engages notions of morality by "intentionally trigger[ing] psychological reactions such as fun, fear, shame, or pride"; in other words, to highlight the benefit and harm of certain decisions to both individuals and the environment (see Text box 3.5).

BOX 3.5 NOTIONS OF BENEFIT AND HARM IN GREEN NUDGES

Green nudges include motivating individuals or groups to compare and compete with one another, with regard to such things as energy and water consumption. Moral persuasion seeks to use ethical arguments in favour of pro-environmental behaviours. It has also been claimed that goal setting and commitments can be used to lock in greener forms of living. Viewed as a whole, Carlsson *et al.* (2021) claim that green nudges that use moral persuasion, because of their explicit targeting of a conscious psychological response, are more likely to be resisted by consumers and are also more likely to lead to a behavioural backlash against pro-environmental behaviours or, in other words, individuals choosing a less environmentally-friendly option if there is a perception that they are being preached at or "guilt-tripped" to act in a certain way. Such claims highlight the difficulty of using notions of benefit and harm in the context of environmental behaviour.

Conclusion

Our aim in this chapter has been to discuss the many contexts in which nudging has been applied in practice over recent years. Nudging, we claim, has been viewed as a popular mechanism to address the many excesses of neoliberalism, doing so in ways that preserves choice while at the same time cajoling individuals to make decisions that improve their health, wealth and happiness and the wellbeing of those around them. Different mechanisms have been employed in different nudges, including the use of choice architectures, the manipulation of time within decision-making, and the promotion of new kinds of social norms. In that sense, there is a considerable breadth to nudging. Nudging as a term masks – even over-simplifies – a whole series of different approaches to changing human behaviour, which are informed by behavioural and psychological insights. As we have stressed throughout this chapter, the nudging "ecosystem" is broad and incredibly varied in character, and it is important for all students of nudging to recognize that.

Our survey of the application of nudging has also reflected on a second theme, namely the limits to nudging. When should public policy make use of behavioural insights and when should more traditional kinds of policy interventions, such as taxes and more punitive laws, be used? There are different ways of answering this question. Some reflect a concern with the effectiveness of nudging as an approach, while others are more ethical in nature. These are themes that we return to in subsequent chapters. But there is a broader, more philosophical, question concerning the limits to nudging. Are all policy challenges ones that could benefit from nudging? Could one, for instance, use nudging as a way of addressing terrorism or misogyny, or racism? The original enthusiasm and potential over-confidence of early proponents of nudging has, perhaps, been replaced by a more mature and reflective approach in which nudging is viewed as one among many kinds of interventions that are required in order to address policy challenges. The mass of evidence that highlights the differing impacts and successes of nudging has, in all likelihood, helped to fuel this more mature approach.

In a different vein, there are much broader implications arising from our discussion in this chapter, namely *who* are the appropriate instigators of nudging interventions? Our discussion has centred mainly on the role played by the state (at different scales) in using nudging to create different kinds of public policy. Some have criticized nudging, in this respect, due to the use made by the state of psychological and behavioural insights that have originated in many instances from the private sector. But is there a difference – should there be a difference – in the way in which the state employs nudging when compared with its use by the private sector? Arguably, ethical and moral issues should be more front and centre when the state uses nudging approaches, more so than they would potentially be in the private sector (Pykett *et al.* 2016). Alternatively, are there other instigators of nudging? Voluntary or third-sector organizations may use nudging to encourage higher levels of charitable donation (Goswami & Urminsky 2016). Individuals can also nudge others or even nudge themselves into different kinds of behaviour. For instance, those wanting to exercise more can nudge themselves to do so by changing into their sportswear as soon as they return home from work instead of doing so just prior to exercising. In all of this, we witness a whole series of issues around the value, the effectiveness and the suitability of nudging in practice.

4

Critiques and controversies

Given its status as a relatively gentle form of power nudging has nevertheless been associated with a surprising number of critiques and controversies. The emergence of nudging policies resulted in the House of Lords' Science and Technology Committee (UK) conducting a thorough review of the relative effectiveness of nudging compared to other behaviour change techniques. The Committee's report also explored the ethics of using nudging techniques and their broader implications for democracy (House of Lords 2011). In the United States, Cass Sunstein's appointment as director of the Office of Information and Regulatory Affairs led radio talkshow host Glenn Beck to describe him as "the most dangerous man in America" (Cole 2014; see also Sunstein 2013). It is perhaps unwise to question too deeply why Beck believed Sunstein (and his nudging ideas) to be so dangerous. Beck's hyperbolic assertion is, however, likely connected to a broader concern that nudging reflects a form of shadowy governmental overreach into personal liberty. In addition to being critiqued from the right, nudging has also been subject to sustained critique from the left. The sociologist Frank Furedi has, for example, suggested that the principles of nudging reflect the latest invocation of elitist notions of false consciousness (2011a; 2011b). In this context, Furedi argues that the practices of nudging rest on the misleading and demeaning assumption that ordinary people do not have the intellectual capacity to know what is in their own best interest and thus require constant moral guidance (2011b).

Critiques of nudging are so numerous and diverse that it is increasingly difficult to discern which concerns are worthy of reflection and which simply reflect a reactionary pile-on mentality. In his *A Manifesto for Applying Behavioural Science* (2023) Michael Hallsworth provides a comprehensive summary of the main concerns that have been raised against the use of behavioural science (and by definition nudging) in public policy (see Text Box 4.1).

In this chapter we shall reflect on these critiques in varying degrees of detail. We shall argue that the veracity of these critiques varies according to which particular form of nudging is being discussed (see Chapters 1 and 2). We have organized these ten critiques into three clusters: (1) underlying science and evidence base; (2) real-world impact; and (3) ethical concerns. The chapter will consider each of these clusters in turn. Ultimately, we argue that the ethical critiques of nudging have proven to be less troubling than their limited real-world impact, a problematic evidence base, and a failure to adequately account for social context. Through a series of case studies, we explore these areas of critique in more detail and reflect upon why nudging appears to have had such a problem with the realities it has encountered.

BOX 4.1 TEN CRITIQUES OF NUDGING

Underlying science and evidence base
Flawed evidence base
Mechanistic thinking
Neglect of social context
Overconfidence
Homogeneity of participants and perspectives (feeding into research)

Real-world impact
Lack of precision
Limited real-world impact
Failure to reach scale

Ethical issues
Ethical concerns (transparency/privacy)
Control paradigm (controlling behaviours of those deemed to be able to control their own)

Source: adapted from Hallsworth (2023).

Science, evidence and nudging's replication crisis

One of the reasons that nudging has been widely adopted by policymakers around the world is the fact that it is grounded on scientific evidence and peer-reviewed studies of human behaviour (see Chapter 2). However, just as nudging was becoming a popular global policy tool, concerns were being raised about its scientific foundations. At the heart of these concerns were questions over the premises of the scientific studies from which nudging emerged and the associated evidence base on which its explanatory power was grounded. One of the prominent sources of anxiety derives from the so-called "replication crisis" in the psychological and behavioural sciences. A key epistemological assumption of science is that the evidence drawn from one study should be able to be reproduced (or replicated) by others using the same methods. But recent studies have demonstrated that many well-established and accepted trials in the psychological and behavioural sciences cannot be replicated (at least not to the same levels of statistical significance). One prominent collaboration published in the journal *Science* replicated 100 psychological trails that had been published in peer-reviewed psychology journals (Open Source 2015). This study was only able to observe the same results in 39 per cent of the replication trials. It appears that the replication crisis is evident in the work of nudge units around the world. In a recent analysis of 126 RCTs conducted by two of the largest nudge units in the United States it was revealed that the average impact of nudges in the real world was much lower than in published academic studies (see DellaVigna & Linos 2022).

It is particularly interesting in the context of nudging to consider what may be causing this replication crisis. According to Konstantin Chatziathanasiou (2022), the replication crisis may itself reflect one of the behavioural biases which nudgers are interested in. Chatziathanasiou (2022) suggests that it is publication bias that may be driving the replication crisis. This publication bias sees prominent journals tending to prioritize the publication of studies with statistically significant results while those not yielding positive results are left in the draws and filing cabinets of scientists. It appears that this bias in publication trends has been exacerbated by a tendency of publishers to showcase novel, "ground-breaking" results, and not studies that seek to prove or disprove existing work. In this context the replication crisis at the heart of nudging's scientific hinterland is itself a product of a bias in publishing which filters out inconclusive results and discourages acts of replicative checking within the scientific community. On these terms, of course, it is important to note that the problems of scientific replication are not unique to the psychological and behavioural sciences but are also a feature of other fields such as medicine. As a relatively new policy tool however, the replication crisis understandably poses more of an existential threat to nudging than medicine. This replication crisis does not, of course, mean that nudging doesn't work. What it does indicate is that nudging is not as reliably effective as many initially believed and that even when nudges do work their effects are not as great as early trials indicated. Chatziathanasiou (2022) observes that this does not mean that we should abandon nudging, rather that the analyses of its costs and benefits needs to be recalibrated. So, if nudging has less reliable positive benefits we need to be careful to ensure that the costs it induces (perhaps in relation to a loss of human autonomy) are still worth the advantages it brings.

In addition to the problems of replication, data fraud has also been identified in at least one scientific publication that has informed nudging policies. A commonly applied nudge is to move honesty statements from the end of forms to the beginning. For example, when completing your tax return it is now common to have to declare a commitment to honesty and accurate declarations (a so-called veracity statement) before you complete the necessary paperwork. The nudge here is premised on the notion of priming people to be honest rather than retrospectively asking if they have been truthful. A key scientific publication which informed this nudge was Shu *et al*.'s (2012) paper "Signing at the beginning makes ethics salient and decreases dishonest self-reports in comparison to signing at the end". Interestingly, this was a study that the authors had struggled to replicate through subsequent trials (see Kristal 2020). On returning to the original study, it was suggested by the authors that there had been a problem of random assignment which had generated a false positive result. Subsequent independent analysis did, however, suggest that the original study may have been based upon fabricated data. While it remains unclear by whom and why this data fabrication was perpetrated, its implications for nudging are likely to be far reaching (Chatziathanasiou 2022). Many governments throughout the world have invested significant time and resources in developing new tax declaration systems that were based on this honesty nudge. Not only did those new systems not yield positive results, but now policymakers have good reason to doubt the veracity of the original science behind these nudging interventions.

It is, perhaps, ironic that it was an honesty-prompting nudge that would expose acts of scientific dishonesty. However, the combination of the replication crisis and data fraud have undermined one of the distinctive features of nudging. Unlike many other policy ideas, nudging was based on clear scientific evidence which was supposed to give policymakers confidence about its real-world efficacy. The science-fuelled confidence associated with nudging speaks to another area of critique surrounding related policy interventions. Namely, concerns over *mechanistic thinking* and the *neglect of social context* within the behavioural sciences. One of the reasons that nudging was seen to be such a powerful tool was because it was supported by the lab-based control trials used by behavioural scientists (see Jones & Whitehead 2018). Within carefully controlled trials, however, social reality can start to look like a machine in which certain inputs produce consistent outputs. But such linear thinking is hard to justify in the context of real-world situations. The issue here relates to broader epistemological criticisms of nudging that emerged from sociology and human geography (see Pedwell 2021; Whitehead *et al.* 2018). Those working at the less (hard) scientific end of the social sciences argued that in separating out human behaviour from social context nudging failed to appreciate the socio-economic structures which form and sustain human behaviours (see Pedwell 2021). The central point in this context is that human action is not determined at the level of observed individual behaviour but was in fact a product of complex social systems and structures which are not evident within control situations. By bracketing out reality behavioural science had been able to provide clear evidence for the effectiveness of nudging, but it ultimately left nudging ill-prepared for its encounters with the real world.

The neglect of social context evident in nudging policies is exemplified well in the Blue Zone Project. The Blue Zone Project is a public health initiative inspired by Dan Buettner's 2012 book *The Blue Zones*.[1] Central to Buettner's analysis was that longevity hotspots (such as Okinawa and Sardinia) were not the result of some form of genetic advantage or superior healthcare system but the social and environmental context of life. The Blue

---

1   The term "blue zones" refers to the colour coding used by demographers to highlight places on the map that have high levels of life expectancy.

Zone Project is a place-based health promotion initiative, which seeks to improve public health in the US (see Carter 2015). It seeks to do this by recreating certain features of life in longevity hotspots, such as high levels of walking, the eating of traditional foods, and the valuing of public space and community engagement.

Eric Carter (2015) argues that the Blue Zone Project is essentially about "health promoting lifestyle management". In this context the project deploys the insights of nudging in a series of ways. According to Carter, Blue Zone Project participants are constantly "nudged" in the direction of better, healthier living, by making small changes to lifestyle and "optimizing" the local environment. The local environment targeted by the project policies is what Buettner calls the "life radius": that "20-mile zone where people spend 80 percent of their time" (Carter 2015: 379). Nudging in the Blue Zone Project focuses in particular on "deconveniencing" everyday life through the provision of improved pavements and cycle lanes and the denormalizing of labour-saving technologies such as leaf blowers. The restructured life radius envisaged within the initiative also seeks to make accessing green/public spaces, healthy food options, and work and schooling easier and thus reduce the need to use the car. Such initiatives are, of course, common features of sustainable city planning and contemporary 15-Minute City schemes. But within the Blue Zone Project Carter argues that nudging becomes a central organizing theme because it is choice environments, and not education, tax or health investments that are the primary policy tools. In this context Carter argues that in a signature nudging move the Blue Zone Project uses "subtle environmental cues to override irrational, irresponsible human behavior" (2015: 279). In this sense, while subtle, the Blue Zone Project could be seen to embody a relatively ambitious form of holistic nudging as the entirety of people's life radius is its target. Through its holistic focus the Blue Zone Project has also been designed to mobilize an additional form of nudging: namely recalibrated social norms and peer pressure (see Carter 2015). The ultimate goal is thus to use changes in choice environments to trigger tipping points in social norms after which car-use and convenience food are seen as socially unacceptable practices.

It may seem strange to choose the Blue Zone Project as an example of the failure of nudging to allow for social context. Compared to many of the initiatives we have considered it is the most holistic and ambitious in its social reach. But this is actually why the Blue Zone Project is such an interesting case of nudging through social context: because even when it is at its best nudging appears to exhibit a very partial and limited view of social context. Table 4.1 outlines the different temporal and spatial scales through which social context can be interpreted within the social sciences (see Whitehead *et al.* 2018). The Blue Zone Project (and the other examples of nudging we have considered throughout this volume) tend to focus on social contexts at the most immediate level of everyday routines (e.g. the food we habitually eat) and individual spatial practices (e.g. how we commute to work). While this context is important, it does not address the wider and longer-term forms of context formation (e.g. how our behaviours may change during our life course, or how the ways in which we connect to where we live takes time to develop). It also fails to address the much longer-term contextual factors, which are much harder to change (eating and exercise norms that are transgenerational and institutionally facilitated) or how our spatial contexts are inherited (it is generally easier to walk to the things we need in the inner city than it is in the suburbs).

None of this is to say that the forms of behaviours that the Blue Zone Project targets are not important. Rather it is to realize that our daily routines and physical environments are not just determined at the local level or by present-day circumstance. Daily behaviours and the environments within which they are enacted are shaped by social processes that transcend the here and now. This does not mean that changes in our everyday practices

Table 4.1 Social context in the social sciences

Contextual temporality	Contextual spatiality
Longue durée Trans-generational practices and institutions	*Institutional spatial practices* Structural and collective production of space
Lifespan Age and stages of life	*Place* Human attachment of meaning to space and the conscious appropriation of surrounding environments
Durée of daily life Routines and habits	*Individual spatial practice* Spatialized habits, physical presence, and routine interaction

Source: Adapted from Simonsen (1991).

71

cannot reshape longer-term contextual factors but rather that changing these behaviours does not necessarily have lasting effects. Nudging's problem with social context should thus not be seen as an oversight but rather as a highly limited understanding of it (see Schatzki 2002; Shove 2013).

However, Carter's critique of the Blue Zone Project, and the nudging it involves, runs deeper than this. According to Carter the limitations of nudging do not just derive from its naïve understandings of the nature of social context, but it also fails to effectively acknowledge the socio-economic and political factors that shape the contexts within which we find ourselves day-to-day. Although the Blue Zone Project recognizes the immediate contextual factors that shape human health, it "[...] promotes a thoroughly desocialized discourse about creating healthy communities. The BZP assiduously avoids contemplation of thorny structural determinants of health, such as income and wealth, educational attainment, employment status, or race and ethnicity" (Carter 2015: 280). For Carter then, nudging is defined by a form of *strategic contextualization*, whereby only those contextual factors that are more easily changed are targeted, while the processes that actually shape context at various scales are largely ignored. This means that attempts to improve public health in US cities seeks to address the contextual barriers to healthy eating and exercise without acknowledging the role of redlining in preventing adequate investment in poor neighbourhoods or recognizing the commercial processes which generate food deserts. Here the methodological limitations associated with the behavioural sciences behind nudging result in it conforming to a neoliberal political agenda (Carter 2015; Jones *et al.* 2013; Whitehead *et al.* 2018). By bracketing out the thorny issues of social context, and the forces that generate inequalities in the contexts we find ourselves in, nudging supports a neoliberal orthodoxy wherein health and well-being are largely determined at a local level, at best, or an individual level, at worst. This, in turn, supports a political agenda of conformism which is opposed to more radical forms of systemic change and redistribution.

Related to these critiques is the issue of *overconfidence*. According to Hans IJzerman *et al.* (2020) overconfidence in the policy claims of behavioural and psychological scientists derives from a (previously mentioned) publication bias and a desire to be taken seriously within governmental circles. But such expressions of confidence are obviously problematic given the scientific and epistemological limitations of the nudging evidence base.

Behavioural public policies like nudges should thus adopt "epistemic humility", particularly in life or death situations such as pandemic and natural disaster responses (IJzerman *et al.* 2020: 1094). Epistemic humility can be secured by engaging both with local experts to test theories and with a broader range of social sciences (Feitsma & Whitehead 2022). IJzerman *et al.* also propose an "evidence readiness level" to assess the values and applicability of a given policy intervention. Inspired by NASA's technology readiness levels, evidence readiness levels seek to introduce a common system for the development and assessment of effective forms of behavioural public policy. In addition to requiring greater engagement with effected communities, the evidence readiness levels proposed by IJzerman *et al.* also seek to encourage so-called "consortium-based research", whereby researchers come together to facilitate the collection of much larger behavioural data sets (akin to what has recently been seen in genetics).

Real-world impacts and spill-over effects

The second broad area of critique concerning nudging relates to its actual-world impacts. Given the issues raised with regard to its evidence base, it is perhaps unsurprising that the *effectiveness* of nudging should also have come under scrutiny. It is important to note that critiques of the real-world impacts of nudging relate not only to failures to deliver public policy benefits. Concerns have also been raised that in certain instances nudges may have generated unanticipated real-world impacts that actually undermine related public policy goals. We shall consider both the lack of positive real-world impacts and the unanticipated presence of negative real-world problems in turn.

The issue of pension savings has been one of the central policy concerns of nudgers (see Thaler & Suntein 2008). It also provides a salutary case study when considering the real-world impacts of nudging. The over-reliance of many pensioners on state benefits and the consistent failure in countries like the US of people to adequately save for retirement has prompted a range of nudging interventions. A central motivation of these interventions is the assumption that the pension crisis can be explained in behavioural terms: namely that it is a product of a collective form of present bias (Chater & Lowenstein 2023). In the context of present bias, a lack of investment in pension schemes is often linked to an individual tendency to prioritize present needs and desires over those of the mid- to long-term future. As we discussed in Chapter 1, a series of nudges have been used both to get people to join company pensions scheme (opt-out defaults) and then to ensure that their levels of investment increase as their salaries increase (so-called auto-escalation). While the use of nudging has increased the number of people on pension schemes it has not been able to address the underlying problems associated with pension savings. According to Chater and Lowenstein (2023), despite the application of nudges pension savings remain stagnant in countries like the UK and US. In the UK nudging hasn't significantly improved pension contribution levels because the default levels of contribution have been set too low, most likely to avoid setting them too high when direct consent has not been given as part of default programmes. Chater and Lowenstein (2023) claim that in this context the use of defaults can actually be counterproductive. While they may be effective at getting people to join pension schemes in the first place, people tend to assume that default contribution settings will meet their long-term pension needs – when in actual fact the default setting is a product of moral expediency and not careful long-term planning. In the US the effectiveness of pension nudges has been eroded by so-called pension "leakage", which occurs when people remove savings from their pension scheme or secure loans against their value. While there are various reasons why people may use their pension savings before retirement, it seems reasonable to assume that they derive mainly from a lack of income. In this context it is clear that the microeconomic practices of nudging depend on favourable macroeconomic circumstances for their success. It is thus significant that auto-escalation schemes have struggled to be effective in the US where amongst poorer demographics wages have remained stagnant (*ibid.*).

There is a final, and perhaps, more significant, reason why nudges have not been successful in addressing the pension crisis. Nudges have been introduced at a time when there has been a major shift in public and private pension schemes from defined benefits to defined contributions schemes (*ibid.*). As the names suggest, defined benefits schemes have specified benefits to pensioners, typically determined by the employee's final salary rate. Defined contributions on the other hand offer a pension determined by how much scheme members decide to pay in, and how well those investments perform. Defined contribution schemes are favoured by pension providers because they shift risk from the provider to the individual scheme member. Under defined contribution schemes it is individuals who must work out what their optimal pension contributions rates should be in order to meet their retirements needs. This, of course, is not an easy task for those who are not pensions experts. And so nudges are deployed as a way to guide scheme members and ensure, through auto-escalation, that their contributions rise along with their incomes. But in this context, we are essentially witnessing nudges being used to support neoliberal pension reforms, which serve to shift the risk, responsibility and blame for the pension crisis onto individuals while ignoring the underlying political and economic causes of pension poverty (see Whitehead *et al.* 2018).

It is important to note the limited effectiveness of nudging in other prominent policy areas. Nudging has been a prominent response to the challenges of getting more people to register as organ donors. Organ donation is a classic behavioural public policy challenge with a majority of people indicating a desire to donate their organs after death, but far fewer actually formally registering to do so. In Wales the devolved government changed the default on organ donation from an opt-in system to a soft opt-out system, where *presumed consent* was given for organ donation unless the person had opted out.[2] Such opt-out organ donation systems have proven successful at increasing the number of people on organ donor registers, but not at actually improving organ transplant rates. The reasons for this are complex. First, to be effective, increasing the number of people on organ donor registers should be paralleled with investment in the logistical systems through which organs can be stored and transported. Second, opt-out systems can generate uncertainty as to the actual intent of a deceased potential donor. As Thaler and Suntein observe, "Under presumed consent, the problem, as we see it, is that it is actually a Families consent policy, and *Families have very little information about donors' wishes*. The fact that someone failed to

2   Interestingly, in their original book, *Nudge*, Thaler and Sunstein (2008) discussed the use of nudging in the context of organ donation. Many people assume that they advocated presumed consent schemes and see related policies that use this tool as a reflection of their policy recommendations. However, Thaler and Sunstein actually supported the use of a so-called "prompted-choice" system. Such as system is used in England where people are given the opportunity to join the organ donor register when they renew their driving licence (for a wider discussion, see Thaler & Sunstein 2021: 253–80).

opt out of some policy may not be very informative, especially if no one is doing so" (2021: 263; original emphasis). In the context of the loss of a loved one, uncertainty over the actual intent of the deceased often leads to families withholding their consent for organ donation. In this real-world situation, families are an important social context within which nudges operate. This is why Thaler and Sunstein prefer the use of prompted-choice nudges as opposed to presumed-consent approaches. The policy choice available to nudgers here does of course remind us of the different forms that nudging can take (see Chapters 1–3). It also emphasizes that not all nudges imply a loss of personal consent.

Perhaps the ineffectiveness of certain nudges relates to their ultimate policy goals. Thus, while nudging appears effective at the initial policy goal of engaging people in pro-social schemes (like company pension programmes and organ donor registers), on its own it cannot address the systemic forces that deliver the ultimate goal (effective saving for retirement and an increase in actual organ transplants). The ineffectiveness of nudging may also relate to the political context within which related policies have been deployed. In the context of austerity within public spending, nudging has been adopted as a relatively cheap policy fix. It has thus seen as a way of avoiding the more costly forms of policy interventions that may be needed to actually deliver policy goals. If nudging could be seen as a policy gateway tool, which could support wider initiatives, there would be perhaps less to worry about in this context. However, there are indications that the use of nudging defaults can actually be counterproductive to the ultimate policy goals of governments.

The counterproductive impacts of nudges lead us directly into the issue of "spillover effects". Spillover effects refer to the unintended consequences of policy interventions, like a nudge. Spillover effects can be negative or positive but are generally unanticipated outcomes of real-world policies. Because spillover effects are not expected they are often unnoticed within the conditions of nudge policy trials. Jonathan Hall and Joshua Madsen (2022) have explored the idea of nudging spillover effects in relation to traffic accident warning signals. Through a study of the impacts of roadside traffic safety nudges in Texas (USA), Hall and Madsen found that roadside signs that indicated the number of crashes on a given stretch of road actually increased rather than decreased the number of accidents. Their explanation for this spillover is interesting because it is anticipated within the behavioural and psychological sciences that inform nudging. They argue that the use of informational nudges on dangerous sections of road generates a form of cognitive overload (particularly when there are likely to be other instructional signs in the same section of road). This cognitive overload, they claim, can generate a form of distraction which increases rather than decreases the chance of a traffic accident.

Steffen Altmann *et al.* (2022) consider the impact of nudges on cognitive resources in more general terms. They claim that in guiding decision-making in certain directions many nudges concentrate attention in certain areas and generate attentional deficits in others. Interestingly, Altmann *et al.* argue that it is educational-style nudges that tend to be the most distracting and place the greatest cognitive load on individuals, while defaults are much less likely to result in cognitive-spillover effects. While not all nudging-spillover effects are necessarily about cognitive overload, this observation does generate an interesting tension when choosing which type of nudge to apply in a given situation. While education/awareness-raising-style nudges may be seen as less manipulative than defaults, defaults may actually result in less cognitive-spillover effects and less unanticipated consequences.

Nudging, ethics and the question of human autonomy

In many ways it is the ethical issues associated with nudging that have been the primary focus of critical analysis. To speak of ethical issues is to raise the fundamental question as to whether it is right, just and fair to be applying nudging techniques within public life. As we shall discuss in this section the ethical issues raised by nudging are not new concerns. They centre on questions of the limits of legitimate state action within society; human freedom, autonomy and tolerance; and moral responsibility. These questions are as old as modern state systems themselves and can be traced back through at least four hundred years of political and moral philosophy (see Runciman 2022). However, we shall also discover that nudging raises novel ethical issues too.

In has been suggested that nudging is unfairly held to higher ethical standards than more orthodox policy mechanisms such as taxation, education and legislation. But there are good reasons why nudging is subjected to ethical scrutiny. At the heart of this seemingly innocuous policy tool are insights that challenge some of the foundations of liberal democratic society. The behavioural sciences that inform nudging challenge many of the assumptions regarding human nature that are at the heart of liberal social norms. According to Rose, within liberal democracy a citizen is conventionally conceived of as: "[…] coherent, bounded, individualised, intentional [entities], the locus of thought, action and belief, the origins of its own actions, [and] the beneficiary of a unique biography" (1998: 3). It is on the basis of assumed human rationality and moral competence that the meritocratic systems of liberal societies rest and associated legal and political systems operate. A belief in citizens' ability to be able to effectively control their own actions and be the locus of their own motivations is key to popular understandings of moral autonomy and our responsibility for our own actions. But, of course, the behavioural sciences behind nudging suggest a very different vision of humans, one that is guided more by their context than an internal moral self, and who are less able to pursue desired behavioural paths than we might assume.

Nudging does not only unsettle our understandings of personal moral responsibility it also draws into question the role of the state within society. As we discussed in Chapter 1, at least since the nineteenth century liberal democracies have broadly sought to limit the role of the state within personal life on the basis of the harm to others principle. As we saw, the harm to others principle states that government intervention within public life is only legitimate when it seeks to prevent the actions of one citizen causing harm to another. The harm to others principle seeks to protect individual citizens' ability to do what they choose in their own life (even if it causes harm to themselves) on the basis that citizens are generally best placed to know their behavioural preferences. The harm to others principle thus suggests that the state has a legitimate role to play in preventing me undermining the health of those around me (perhaps through smoking in an enclosed space), but should not prevent me from compromising my own health (through smoking alone). The soft power of nudging does, however, suggest that it may be possible to address harm-to-self issues without undermining the freedom of citizens, who if the nudge has been well-designed should be easily able to resist it (Sunstein 2019).

Beyond these broad moral and constitutional issues, nudging has become synonymous with a series of more specific ethical debates. Given that many (but by no means all) nudges target unconscious biases, nudging has been accused of forms of manipulation that are difficult to discern and thus resist

(Jones *et al.* 2013; White 2013). Legislation and related forms of paternalism may be more coercive expressions of government than nudges, but they can generally be perceived and thus resisted or contested. It is argued that nudging's gentle nature belies a form of manipulation which is insidious. In response to these concerns the UK's House of Lords argued that nudges should be as transparent and easily discernible as is feasible (2011). Given that many nudges appear to work best when they are not perceived by those who are subjected to them, transparency may not always be possible to achieve. Some critics of nudges have also questioned the ways in which related policies tend to equate choice with both freedom and consent. Even the most rudimentary ethical analysis of nudging would have to concede that actively choosing to do something is very different from being subconsciously guided to follow a particular course of action. In this context, Furedi (2011a) suggests that nudging represents an assault on tolerance within public life. Tolerance can take different forms including a tolerance of a right to be wrong. But it can also be discerned in the option not to have to choose. Thus, when the renewal of a driving licence requires that a decision on whether to join an organ donor register is made, it could be claimed that this reflects an act of intolerance, by making it morally difficult to choose a course of action that may be perceived as selfish or socially unacceptable (see Chapter 1).

In response to the issue of being forced to choose advocates of nudging would point to the fact that many people want to join organ donor registers but simply never get around to this. Prompted, or mandated, choice is thus justified on the basis of enabling a significant portion of the population to achieve their behavioural goals. This perspective does, however, raise another issue with regard to nudges: the issue of asymmetry. Nudging is often justified on the basis that it is asymmetrically paternalist (see Chapter 2). In other words, it helps those who need and want help in changing their behaviours, but it does not force the hand of those who do not need help or do not want to change their behaviours (Lowenstein *et al.* 2007). However, being forced to choose may not only affect the segments of the population it is targeted at. It may also involve a moral cost for those who have to now make a choice on an issue. The House of Lords (2011) sought to address this concern by arguing that nudges are legitimate if they have a high level of social acceptability. Whereas nudges that exhibit symmetrical forms of paternalism could be seen to embody, what Mill termed, the tyranny of the majority: an anathema to liberal society. The House of Lords' findings also rightly pointed out that governments have a role to play in supporting policy that shift behaviours in ways that are initially not widely supported by the public. If nudges are seen to involve unacceptable forms of manipulation, then their capacity to be used in areas without widespread public support could be limited.

A significant line of critical inquiry into the impacts of nudging has been developed by political scientists, which moves from a concern with manipulation and personal autonomy to consider the wider implications of nudging for political subjectivities and wider democratic systems (see Button 2018; Leggett 2014). Mark Button's work is significant in this context as it explores the connection between the assumptions of bounded human rationality associated with nudging and the subsequent "bounding of democracy" within the political sphere (2018). Reflecting on the practices of a "nudging-state", Button raises concerns that while such forms of intervention may be justified in terms of welfare, they have potentially negative connotations for political agency and civic capacity (2018: 1035). Button argues that the normalization and widespread use of nudging could be detrimental for political agency. In particular, he reflects upon the tendency of nudging policies to emanate from unelected behavioural experts, and to focus on individual as opposed to collective action issues. Nudge-type policies, he argues, fail to perceive subjects as citizens engaged in public life and collective acts of freedom. Making decision-making easier (by often removing the cognitive burden of having to think and deliberate about them) may make sense in relation to individual wellbeing, but when it comes to politics getting more actively involved in, and even contesting, courses of action is rather the point of being political. Button thus observes, "[…] citizens in their public capacity as agents of political freedom are missing from the latest integration of behavioral science and public policy" (2018: 1040). There are, therefore, two primary aspects of Button's critique. First, is the notion that nudging militates against the development of active citizens who are engaged in the collective political process. Second, is a concern with the way in which the goals of policy are determined by behavioural experts in a post-political process outside of mainstream politics.[3]

---

3   For a wider discussion of the connections between nudging and post-politics, which challenges Button's perspective, see Whitehead *et al.* (2020).

Despite the significance of such critiques there are no necessary reasons why nudging has to undermine the democratic political process and notions of active citizenship. As Button observes, "One of the advantages of taking the behavioral sciences seriously within the design and conduct of democratic deliberative practices is that we can purchase greater psychological realism without sacrificing democratic aspirationalism" (2018: 1043). Here Button essentially recognizes that nudging can be helpful in enabling us to recognize that there may be cognitive and behavioural reasons why people do not take a more active role in the democratic process (very few of us will conform to the idealized vision of the wise Athenian citizens upon which many of our democratic assumptions still rest). In this context, it is possible to imagine nudging people into more active forms of collective deliberation and action – combining *psychological realism* with *democratic aspirationalism*.

The use of nudging to promote more engaged forms of citizenship has been a central part of the "Nudge and Think" and "Nudge plus" approaches to public policy (see John *et al.* 2011; Banerjee & John 2021). These approaches have explored the ways in which nudging can be used to bring people into politics. In a narrow sense this can involve the use of nudging to promote voter turn-out in elections, but in more general terms as a prompt for people to think more deeply about social issues and to participate in deliberate decision-making processes. According to Peter John *et al.*, "The nudge strategy accepts citizens as they are, and tries to divert them down new paths to make better decisions [whereas] the think strategy has a different account of what makes humans tick. It assumes that the individual can step away from the day-today experience, throw off their blinkers and reflect on the wide range of policy choices and dilemmas" (2011: 19). The strategic combination of nudging people to think and participate in democratic processes combines realism with idealism in an undeniably attractive way. It also reflects a distinct shift in the methodology of nudging, with nudges being used to prompt more conscious forms of deliberation about and engagement within politics and social issues. The extent to which these approaches can be effectively balanced, however, remains an open question.

Conclusion

Within this chapter we have considered the major critiques and concerns that have been levelled at nudging (see Table 4.2 for a summary). These concerns fall into two main areas: do nudges actually work? And can they be applied in ethical and non-manipulative ways? Many of the ethical concerns raised about nudges have proven to be unfounded. Public-sector nudges have generally been carefully applied and managed by governments and have remained relatively easy to resist. However, the effectiveness of nudges has remained a concern, particularly in the context of the replication crisis and accusations of data fraud.

Interestingly, Chatziathanasiou (2022) argues that the ethical assessment of the value of nudges must take into account their relative levels of effectiveness. So, a highly effective nudge, delivering clear social benefit may be deemed to be ethically more acceptable even if it lacks transparency than a less effective nudge which is highly transparent. In this context it is important to consider the critiques of nudging in relation to each other and to assess the overall proportional value of nudges accordingly: this is

Table 4.2 The pros and cons of nudging

Pro-nudge	Anti-nudge
Clear social benefit	Who decides what is a social good?
Unregulated commercial social influence already exists (sludge)	It is manipulative and hard to resist – uses human frailties against us
Can preserve choice	Reduces freedom of choice – what of our right not to choose?
Helping people help themselves	Issues of tolerance and right to be wrong
Can be effective in specific circumstances	Does not address underlying social drivers of problems
Maintains democratic accountability	Takes unnecessarily pessimistic view of human nature
Related policies being held to a higher ethical standard?	Too narrow in focus on how to change behaviours (non-regulatory)
Rigorous scientific evidence base	Replication crisis and data fraud

essentially a calculation of efficacy and ethics. The following chapter will consider how the transition of nudging to online, corporate platforms has radically transformed both the effectiveness and ethics of nudging. In this context we shall consider how nudging appears to have become more effective and ethically problematic at the same time.

5

The digital future of nudging

Ed Bradon (2022) has suggested that despite being with us for over decade we have only scratched the surface of what nudging could do as a policy tool. In the context of the still limited rollout of nudging and the fact that the vast majority of attempts to change and reform people's behaviour are unsuccessful, Bradon argues that in the future we would be foolish not to explore the potential benefits of nudging more widely. In this chapter we consider what the future of nudging may look like. Critically we claim that the future power of nudging is likely to be more significant than it has been in the past, and that its future iterations will likely raise new and more troubling ethical and political issues than its older forms.

In broad terms there are a series of future trajectories that nudging could take. First, it could diminish in popularity and fade from use as other policy techniques have done in the past. We think that this is unlikely. Second, it may gradually grow in significance and become an accepted part of behaviour changing programmes in the public and private sectors. We think that this trajectory is more likely, but only really tells part of the future story of nudging. There is a third direction of travel: one which sees nudging undergo radical transformation in both its reach and functionality to become a very significant source of power and influence. It is this third trajectory that provides the focus for this chapter. It is our contention that nudging has already radically transformed (one may even say mutated) and is playing a much more significant role in our lives they we may realize.

The last 20 years have witnessed a series of experimental fusions between the data and behavioural sciences. These developments go by many names. Shoshana Zuboff (2015, 2016, 2019) has described these developments in terms of "surveillance capitalism" and the emergence of a whole new brand of economics devoted to the digital monitoring and shaping of human behaviours (see Text Box 5.1). Others have labelled these developments as "micro-", "continuous-" or "hyper"-nudging (see Yeung 2019; Whitehead & Collier 2022: 75–98). What these different terms collectively capture are particular forms of *digitized* nudging. The digitization of nudging has not simply seen the delivery of nudging through digital devices or on online platforms. The digitization of nudging has also involved fundamental changes in the functional potential and DNA of the nudge (Mills 2022). As more of our lives have moved online, and increasingly large segments of our existence are now exposed to digital monitoring, the potential development and application of bespoke nudging interventions at very large scales (we are talking here of hundreds of millions, if not billions, of people) has grown significantly. Indeed, the history of nudging is a story that runs in connected parallel to the concomitant rise of the smart-tech digital world (see Whitehead & Collier 2022). Although we may not realize it, the future of nudging may already be here.

This chapter begins by considering the nature and origins of digital nudging. In the second section we outline the different forms that digital nudging can take and consider specific examples of their applications. This takes us on a journey through Facebook's involvement in political elections, Capitol One's attempts to deliver bespoke financial products, and Instagram's attempts to limit harmful online behaviours. The final section considers the controversies and concerns that surround the widespread commercial application of digital nudges.

The nature and origins of digital nudging

Kahneman's algorithmic turn

In 2009, the year after the publication of Thaler and Sunstein's *Nudge*, Daniel Kahneman, the grandfather of behavioural economics, made a telling observation which pre-empted the contemporary alliance between data sciences and nudging. In an article for the journal *American Psychologist* (co-authored with Gary Klein) Kahneman observed, "The idea of algorithms that outdo human judges is a source of pride and joy for the HB (Heuristics and Biases) tribe […] There is compelling evidence that under certain conditions mechanical and analytical judgements outperform human judgements" (Kaheman & Klein 2009: 523). Kahneman and Klein go on to advocate the superiority of algorithms over humans in making medical prognoses and improving the risk assessments associated with the awarding of personal loans.[1]

We should, of course, not be surprised that Kahneman would be so excited about the prospects of algorithms. In his pioneering work on biases, Kahneman identified what he saw to be the irredeemable limitations of human decision-making, paving the way for nudging (see Chapter 2). Kahneman's evident pride and joy at the potential utility of algorithms is clearly because he sees their operation as a kind of technological proof of concept for his work. As technological versions of *Homo economicus*, algorithms demonstrate what rational decision-making in the real world should look like, while exposing the errors of even expert human judgements. The operation of algorithms could, in this context, be seen as a justification for the use of nudging: humans struggle to cope with complex decision-making environments, but algorithms could provide rapid guides to optimal courses of action, which could be transmitted, in real time, through nudges.

In retrospect there are two important reflections we can make on Kahneman's enthusiasm for algorithms. First, we now know that far from being cybernetic *Homo economicuses*, algorithms are also burdened with biases. Their recent use in various sectors has, for example, revealed that they exhibit gender, racial and class-based biases. Second, back when Kahneman and Klein wrote their article, the potential use of algorithms to support more optimal human decision-making was constrained. There were still relatively limited amounts of digital data available to feed into algorithms in order to enable them to make their mechanical calculations. Additionally, there were inadequate routes through which optimized algorithmic insights could be relayed to use in the form of digital nudges (smart phones and devices were still limited in their use and availability). Since Kahneman and Klein's celebration of the algorithmic in 2009 there has, of course, been an

---

1 Interestingly, while Kahneman and Klein emphasize the superiority of algorithms over human decision-making, they acknowledge that the available evidence does not suggest that algorithms are flawless or that humans are irredeemably bad at decision-making. They acknowledge that algorithms are most useful when decision-making environments give weak or limited clues as to what is happening. Even in these contexts algorithms get things wrong and when given discernible signals human judgement can be very reliable.

unprecedented fusion of the behavioural and data sciences. This merger has occurred at the same time as the digitization of everyday life and has enabled algorithms to absorb more and more data about our lives and society, which is then fed back to people in the form of digital prompts. In the remainder of this section, we consider the particular nature of the connections that have been made between the data and behavioural sciences and how these have produced very particular understandings of the human and behavioural influence within the Big Tech sector.

Forms of digital nudging: micro-, hyper- and intimate-nudging

The new era of digital nudging is predicated on two developments. First is the digitization of everyday life and work. The internet, social media platforms and satellite navigation has meant that much more of our life is expressed and recorded in digital forms. Shopping, socializing, travelling and exercising are now increasingly being mediated by digital devices, which make our lives easier, but also easier to monitor. In addition, an increasing number of government services – from tax returns to passport applications – are now moving onto digital-first systems. Digital nudging involves taking advantage of the digital choice environments many of us now inhabit as a context to deliver behavioural change (Jesse & Jannach 2021). Second, is the emergence of smart technology not just in phones, but in cars, fridges, watches and even vacuum cleaners (Whitehead & Collier 2022). These devices have the ability to learn about our lives and provide feedback that can shape and change our online and offline behaviours. These interconnected developments have contributed to two branches of digital nudging.

The first generation of nudges to enter the digital realm focused on digital prompts and the reshaping of digital choice environments. Given that nudging emerged towards the end of the first decade of the twenty-first century, these forms of digital nudges are as old as nudging itself. Nudging as a form of digital prompt utilizes digital devices as delivery systems for messages that encourage certain forms of behaviour (this could involve, for example SMS messages encouraging us to complete our tax returns on time, or emails reminding us to give blood). Digital prompts can be considered nudges when they can easily be avoided and seek to either address or utilize behavioural biases as a way of delivering some form of social benefit or improved service (Weinmann *et al.* 2016). These forms of digital nudge have certain advantages over analogue nudges. First, it is much easier for them to instantly reach large segments of the population at relatively low cost. The use of direct mail or print adverts to deliver nudging prompts is, in this context, more time consuming and far more expensive. Simple digital prompts can also more easily incorporate some degree of segmentation (or what behavioural economists would call *asymmetry*), with only those who the message is relevant to receiving the nudge (so if you have filed your tax return you are not subject to generic nudges that are targeted at those who have not). Finally, it is much easier to tweak and change digital prompting nudges if they prove ineffective.

Early iterations of digital nudging also sought to reshape digital choice environments. These forms of digital nudging focus on user interface design as a way to shape and guide our choice (Weinmann *et al.* 2016). Recognition of the potential role of digital technologies to shape behaviours at the user interface does, of course, predate nudging. In Chapter 2 we discussed the pioneering work of Donald Norman in the field of cognitive design, and how his analysis of the Unix operated systems revealed the unhelpful cognitive loads it placed on users. The later work of B. J. Fogg at Stanford explored how the rise of ubiquitous computing provided the opportunity to deploy computers as forms of persuasive behavioural technologies (Fogg 1998). The reshaping of digital choice architectures reflects an attempt to fuse the insights of cognitive design and persuasive computing with the insights of behavioural psychology. Reshaped digital choice architectures can deliver nudges in a series of ways. They may, for example, make it easier for users to do things – as in the case of the prepopulated online tax forms now used by the revenue authorities in the UK. Digital user interfaces also make it easier for nudgers to practice choice editing: perhaps simplifying a choice by highlighting a popular or previously chosen option, or by mandating that a choice be made before a task can be completed.

Within digital choice environments it is also much easier to deploy three powerful nudging tools: peer pressure, default resetting and loss aversion. On many social media platforms nudging is now pursued by deliberately revealing to the user who among their peer group has already pursued a particular course of action (perhaps voting in an election or joining a weight-loss programme). Within a range of digital systems, it is also easier to reset defaults so as to promote pro-social behaviours. Weinmann *et al.*

(2016: 433) for example, note that the app Square now sets tipping for service as a default with the effect of increasing the amount of tips received for services rendered. A final, if controversial, application of nudging on digital platforms has seen hotel booking sites deploy loss aversion techniques. In this context, it has become common for such sites to not only reveal details of the hotel rooms which are being booked, but also the number of people who are looking at the room and how many rooms remain available. Signalling to consumers the popularity of a product and the need to avoid the loss of an in-demand room is a potentially beneficial digital nudge. It transpires, however, that certain sites were using loss aversion nudges in a misleading way: for example, flags like "only five rooms remaining" related only to the rooms in a particular hotel that were available on a given platform, others may well have been available through other booking services. It is clear that the emergence of digital nudging has generated new opportunities for the deployment of "sludge" (the use of behavioural insights to promote behaviours that may be in the best interest of the nudger, not the nudged; see Chapter 2).[2]

The second generation of digital nudging utilizes digital infrastructures in more immersive ways. These types of nudges were first identified and named by the legal scholar Karen Yeung. Yeung described how, over the past decade, a new form of digital nudging has risen to prominence that seeks to make use of digital technology, algorithms and smart devices. She described these practices as "hyper-nudging". According to Yeung, hyper-nudging involves:

> [...] configuring and thereby personalizing the user's informational choice context, typically through algorithmic analysis of data streams from multiple sources claiming to offer predictive insights concerning the habits, preferences and interests of targeted individuals (such as those used by online consumer product recommendation engines), these nudges channel user choices in directions

---

2 Interestingly, in their updated version of *Nudge*, Thaler and Sunstein (2022) reflect on the way in which sludge can emerge at the intersection of the analogue and digital: with the easy to use digital systems of purchase and subscription, comparing unfavourably to more labourious analogue systems for unsubscribing or product return.

> preferred by the choice architect through processes that are subtle, unobtrusive, yet extraordinarily powerful.   (Yeung 2016: 119)

A key difference, therefore, between first-generation digital nudging and hyper-nudging is the fact that hyper-nudging does not only use digital systems to transmit nudges to people. Hyper-nudging also exploits the emerging infrastructure of what Zuboff calls "surveillance capitalism" in order to learn about the targets of nudging and to tailor highly personalized and bespoke nudges. We shall outline in more detail the form that hyper-nudging can take below, but it is evident in the construction of our social media feeds, the results of our Google searches and even in predictive text systems.

Hyper-nudging is dependent on two entities for its operation: the algorithm and the smart device. As discussed in the previous sections, algorithms are important to hyper-nudging because they are able to compute the large amounts of digital data that reflect our daily activities into meaningful patterns, which can provide insights into who we may like to befriend, what we may like to buy, which films we would like to watch, and the political orientation we prefer in the news apps we use. If algorithms can help us navigate complex decision-making, it is smart devices and technologies that gather the data on which hyper-nudging depends. The example of the smart watch demonstrates the connection between smart technology and hyper-nudging. Smart watches are now able to continuously monitor a range of aspects of our everyday life, including changing heart rates, exercise activities, the number of steps we take and stairs we climb. Information about an individual can be stored, monitored and used to nudge future exercise patterns. Smart watches can buzz to remind us to stand-up if we have been sedentary for too long, send us a message if our exercise level is down in comparison to the previous day, and congratulate us on the successful meeting of activity or sleep goals (Whitehead & Collier 2022: 99–126). Smart devices are thus critical to the operation of the hyper-nudge because they both facilitate the gathering of the information that such nudges depend on and because they offer the vehicle for delivering the final nudge. The gathering and storing large amounts of data about our daily activities can also facilitate the opportunity for users to consciously reflect on their personal health and wellbeing. Of course, the digital form of this personalized data means that it can easily be shared with third-parties so that broader patterns of behaviour can be discerned and the impacts of nudging assessed. While hyper-nudging should not strictly involve financial incentives for action, many life and health insurance companies now offer better premiums if we open ourselves up to smart-tech data gathering and the practices of digital nudging. Hyper-nudging could also very easily transform into more coercive/regulatory forms: as our smart fridge locks itself in support of our dietary efforts or our smart car automatically deactivates if we have not paid our insurance.

Voice-activated technology such as Apple's Siri or Amazon's Alexa are now becoming key vectors for the delivery of hyper-nudges. These devices deepen the intimate nature of digital nudging as they are able to calibrate their response in relation to the user's voice tone and relay nudges through a reassuring and familiar voice.

As with all nudges, hyper-nudges can take many different forms, but it is important to recognize that hyper-nudging can often overlap with other behaviour change mechanisms (see Figure 5.2). It is interesting to think about the operation of hyper-nudges in relation to Simon's notion of bounded rationality (see Chapter 2). In Simon's scissors model of bounded rationality human decision-making is limited both by the cognitive bandwidth of our thoughts and the inevitable limitations of the decision-making environments we find ourselves in. Analogue nudges address bounded rationality by focusing on the environmental blade of Simon's scissors and redesigning choice architectures to guide behaviour in more optimal directions. Hyper-nudges, however, are unique to the extent that they target both the cognitive and environmental sources of our constrained rationalities.

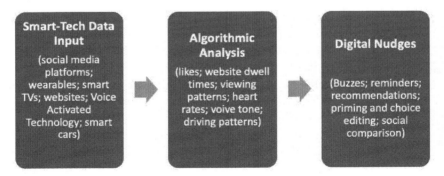

Figure 5.1 The hyper-nudge process

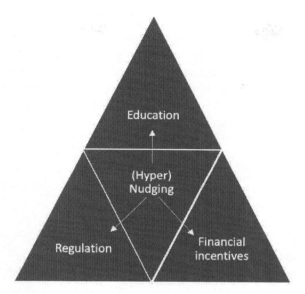

Figure 5.2 Hyper-nudging in relation to more traditional policy instruments

Within the hyper-nudge system described above, the combination of the knowledge-gathering capabilities of digital/smart technology and the power of algorithms (and potentially AI) promises an elevated cognitive potential that can discern optimal courses of action more easily. In this context, the choice architect is no longer human, but a digital system that can guide action in highly individualized ways. Hyper-nudges can also continually reshape our choice environment. This may involve redesigning the online systems and platforms we use to optimize choice, or the relaying of in-situ nudges through the smart devices that are embedded in our lives. On these terms, hyper-nudges appear to be very different from their more static analogue relatives. However, it is important to consider more systematically what distinguishes hyper-nudges from analogue nudging.

According to Stuart Mills (2022) hyper-nudging does not reflect a new type of nudge per se, but rather a change in the system through which nudges occur. Hyper-nudges still rely on the same fundamental approaches to behaviour change as nudges: namely the mobilization of social norms, loss aversion, status quo bias and the restructuring of choice. According to Mills, however, the new system of nudging associated with the hyper-nudge means that it does reflect a much more significant evolution of nudging than is evident in first-generation digital nudging. What distinguishes hyper-nudging from nudging is the highly personalized and experimental form it takes. The analogue nudge involved reconfiguring choice environments (whether that be a tax form or work canteen) and then testing how effective that reconfiguration was in achieving a particular behavioural goal (increasing tax compliance, healthier eating, etc.). These forms of nudges were limited by two factors: (1) the time that it took to implement the redesign of the choice architecture (not so long with a tax form, but much longer with a healthy dining initiative); and (2) limited insights into how effective the nudge had been (expressed in aggregate percentage changes in targeted behaviour). The hyper-nudge system on the other hand has the ability to effortlessly produce a continuous stream of changes in our choice environments and to immediately assess the impact related nudges have had on individual behaviours.

What emerges, according to Mills (2022), is a form of nudging which is able to follow the subject around, testing which nudges work best, in which context, and even at which times of day. Within this system there is not even any need for a behavioural theory to inform a nudge. Rather than seeing how suspectable a person is to a reset default, algorithms can simply reset a randomized feature of choice architecture to see the behavioural results it yields (Zuboff 2019). Mills (2022) and Yeung (2016) compare the hyper-nudge to the speed hump/bump (or "sleeping policeman/woman" in the UK). The speed bump is a kind of nudge which does give us the choice of whether we wish to slow down or not (or at least how much we wish to slow down). As an analogue nudge, the speed bump is distinct from the hyper-nudge in three key ways: (1) it is applied to everyone using the street in the same way (even the emergency services have to slow down to some extent); (2) its impact on each driver's behaviour is not measured (instead the aggregate impact of the bump on average traffic speeds will, perhaps, be studied); and (3) the speed bump does not follow individual drivers around (see Mills 2022). So hyper-nudges have clear advantages. Hyper-nudges do not need to be applied to everyone, thus avoiding any adverse effects, or inconveniences, caused by nudging being experienced by those who do not benefit from them. Hyper-nudges are also normally able to immediately measure the impact of a nudge and to assess whether it is worth deploying again in the future.

Hyper-nudges do, of course, raise a series of concerns. The fact that hyper-nudges can follow users around and generate ever more personalized behavioural prompts makes them potentially inescapable. The perpetual enrolment of users to behavioural experiments, of which they are often unaware, has been described as a form of "guinea pig economy" (Jones & Whitehead 2018). Indeed, it is likely that at times nudge experiments will not be oriented to a particular goal but merely to facilitate learning about the impacts that they can have. The fact that many nudges are being deployed by Big Tech companies (such as Google, Amazon and Facebook) also raises the question of their commercial orientation. As we shall show in the next section, it is in this context that the connections between hyper-nudges and surveillance capitalism become significant. Although hyper-nudges may be oriented towards pro-social forms of behaviour, they are nonetheless able to feed the learning loops of surveillance capitalism and support the commercial exploitation of human behaviour by the Big Tech sector (see Whitehead & Collier 2022; Zuboff 2019). In providing deeper insights into individual preferences and susceptibility to particular behavioural prompts, hyper-nudges can easily move from a situation where they are enabling users to pursue their behavioural preferences, to actually developing preferences to suit commercial ends. This is perhaps the tension that characterizes hyper-nudging: the costs of a more sophisticated, bespoke and effective system of nudging are that it is locked into a capitalist system that seeks the commercial exploitation of behavioural manipulation. If, as Mills (2022) argues, hyper-nudging is more a system of nudging than merely a type of nudge, then it clearly raises questions about whether hyper-nudging should be seen as a gentle form of power. Hyper-nudges' adaptability and continuous application clearly indicate the potential for a more insidious and powerful system of behavioural influence.

BOX 5.1 SURVEILLANCE CAPITALISM

The idea of "surveillance capitalism" was developed by the American academic Shoshana Zuboff. In her 2019 book *The Age of Surveillance Capitalism*, Zuboff described surveillance capitalism as "[a] new economic order that claims human experience as free raw material for hidden commercial practices of extraction, prediction, and sales" (2019: ix). Surveillance capitalism has emerged as the dominant regime of accumulation associated with Big Tech giants like Facebook/Meta, Amazon, Google, and increasingly Microsoft. This is a capitalist system which is not focused on the exploitation of the natural world (as with nineteenth-century industrial capitalism) or, primarily, with the sale of products (as with mid- to late-twentieth-century Fordism), but instead seeks to better understand, predict and exploit human behaviour. In this new economic era monopolies are not defined by the production of goods and services, but by the highly uneven division of knowledge and learning. On these terms, Zuboff claims that surveillance capitalism is a "[…] rogue mutation of capitalism marked by concentrations of wealth, knowledge, and power unprecedented in human history" (*ibid*.). Surveillance capitalism thus helps to explain how many Big Tech companies generate wealth while offering many of their services for free.

The origins of surveillance capitalism can be discerned in the emergence of Web 2.0 platforms and the relatively low levels of regulation that Big Tech companies were subjected too following 9/11 and their enrolment in state-based surveillance systems. The original model of surveillance capitalism was, according to Zuboff, "Googlenomics" which is based on the realization that money could be made from the so-called "behavioural surpluses" that we all generate when we use digital technology (behavioural surpluses are those previously unused forms of data about our habits, preferences, views and likes that we leave like breadcrumbs on websites and digital platforms). Google combined its vast behavioural surplus data with its data analytic power to be able to make and sell predictions about user's needs. Zuboff observes that "behavioural surplus was the game changing, zero-cost asset that was diverted from service improvement [search quality] towards a genuine and lucrative market exchange" (2019: 81). Of course, with the emergence of embedded smart tech and the Internet of Things, it is now possible to gather behavioural surpluses not only from so-called "web crawling", but also through *life crawling*.

Surveillance capitalism in not, however, just about what Zuboff terms data *rendition*, it is also concerned with behavioural *actuation*. Behavioural actuation seeks to use the insights gleaned from our behavioural data surpluses to actually shape decisions and behaviour. This, according to Zuboff, is where (hyper-)nudges come into play (2019: 294–5). Zuboff describes how surveillance capitalism uses nudges (and the behaviouralist tactics of *herding*, *tuning* and *conditioning*) to generate behaviour change. Within surveillance capitalism nudges can be used to promote personal and social wellbeing (while still generating commercial revenue), but surveillance capitalism has seen the widespread privatization of nudging (Whitehead 2020). Within this act of privatization nudging is now commonly used to support the commercial needs of Big Tech and others over and above the needs of those who are being nudged (Zuboff 2019: 295). The privatization of nudging is a particular concern in the context of the power and reach of Big Tech and the ways that hyper-nudges often circumvent human consciousness. Zuboff's theory of surveillance capitalism reveals that hyper-nudging may be removing many of the ethical guardrails associated with analogue nudges and undermining the human capacity to resist and contest even gentle forms of behavioural power.

Digital nudges in action

There are three broad types of digital/hyper nudging (see Figure 5.3). The first seeks to shape choice in complex knowledge environments (for example, choosing a financial product like a pension scheme). The second utilizes nudges to prompt desired public and private behaviours (perhaps the observation of public health mandates in the midst of a pandemic). The third focuses primarily on mitigating the worst effects of digital life and surveillance capitalism. As we discuss below, related nudges can be used to support public policy goals (financial security, health and wellbeing, and environmental protection) and narrower commercial interests (the sale of products and the reputational protection of corporations). Digital nudges can be delivered by public bodies but are more commonly administered by private companies sometimes acting in partnership with governments.

The first type of digital nudging utilizes the knowledge gathering and analytical capabilities associated with surveillance capitalism to guide user decision-making. It is interesting to note in this context, that many of those who design human/digital interfaces are well versed in the insights of behavioural economics and nudging techniques (see Whitehead & Collier 2022). Choice editing and guidance in complex knowledge situations can be discerned in a range of everyday digital contexts, including the ordering of Google search results, what is on our Facebook newsfeed, and the dynamic advice offered by satellite navigation systems. In each of these situations, knowledge is presented in suggestive, but non-coercive, ways. If you are not pleased with what your Google search returns, scroll down further, or refine your search terms; should you disagree with your sat nav, then just ignore it. These are all forms of digital nudging because they provide a

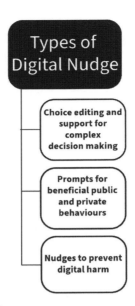

Figure 5.3 Types of digital nudge

choice architecture within which we are free to choose the information we wish to focus on from the plethora of options that are available. But all use gentle and non-coercive forms of influence.

The broader utility of digital nudging within complex digital knowledge environments is discussed by Chris Risdon (2017).[3] Risdon was previously Head of Behavioural Design at the finance company Capital One and his interests are in the fusion of nudging and algorithms. In a piece for *Behavioral Scientist* entitled "Nudges with Machine Learning" he outlined some of the ways that nudging could be used to help people make wiser financial decisions. He discerns three primary benefits to hyper-nudging within the financial sector: (1) they algorithmically determine the best financial product for users (through an ability to be able to assess data on personal needs, financial product performance, and the actual performance of different financial products for large numbers of users); (2) they are able to determine the ideal rates of contributions that individuals should make

---

3   For a more detailed discussion of Risdon's analysis, see Whitehead and Collier (2022: 87–8).

to financial products (such as saving accounts); and (3) the insights of the calculations that inform hyper-nudging can be easily scaled-up to potentially millions of users, thus bringing benefits to a wide population and enhancement to the financial performance of a company's products. It is particularly interesting in the context of our previous discussion of the history of nudging (see Chapter 2), to see how Risdon describes the operation of hyper-nudges in the financial sector:

> The implication is that if people invite positive influence, we need to scale our ability to influence them, not just through marketing and acquisition, but the entire product or service lifestyle [...] It's a two-part challenge. Augment the person's rational self by providing a decision engine that, using machine learning, finds insightful patterns in their life [...] Then, control a person's irrational self: identify and target their unique combination of biases and heuristics they use to make decisions, and protect them from those biases.
>
> (2017: 3)

In this context it is clear that within hyper-nudges there is an attempt to both circumvent the limitations of System 2 thinking (to boost rationality) and to simultaneously inhibit the irrational interference of System 1 instincts and biases (to counteract irrationality). Of course, to some extent this has always been the purpose of nudging, as a choice architect determines welfare enhancing types of behaviour and seeks to achieve them by both exploiting and controlling human irrationality. Within the hyper-nudge, however, the machine-learning algorithm replaces the human choice architect and develops much more bespoke calculations of optimal behavioural trajectories and the identification of personalized nudging techniques that can best target our irrationalities. Risdon actually compares the hyper-rational potential of digital nudges to medical breakthroughs in genetics: "Just like unlocking the human genome helped identify genetic traits that allow for personalized medical advice, we can think of machine learning as the next step in unlocking a 'behavior genome,' by factoring in personality traits, situational features, and timing, we can better persuade people who want to be persuaded" (*ibid.*: 6).

In this context, the purported significance of hyper-nudging is not just to be found in its ability to continuously nudge historically unprecedented numbers of people (perhaps through the resetting of personal saving level defaults; or the auto-escalation of pension saving contributions). The true significance of hyper-nudging is based on the power of its underlying algorithms to discern courses of action that can realistically lead to the achievement of different people's life goals (perhaps funding a child's education, or an early retirement). It is not only about nudging people in a (predetermined) direction; it is about the bespoke calculation of what that direction can realistically be. In this context, hyper-nudges promise to present us with future lifestyle options our bounded rationality prevents us from even perceiving, never mind achieving!

The second type of nudging involves the use of prompts for beneficial public and private behaviours. These prompts could be the buzz of a smart watch to inform us we have exercised less than the previous day; a message from Duo Lingo that informs us we have met our language learning goal for the week; or, perhaps, our smart phone checking that we are not driving before we unlock our home screen while in a car. These nudges can be informed by big data analysis and the machine-learning algorithms associated with the choice editing digital nudges described above. Most likely, however, they reflect relatively simple digital nudges that are based on comparison with our previous behaviours (our smart watch fitness reminder), or goals and defaults we have set for our own behaviours (as with a language learning app goal or Blue Tooth enabled smart phone locks). Related nudges can be fairly innocuous at an individual level, but they can be used in broader public contexts where they can once again raise thorny ethical issues. A case in point is Facebook's Voter Megaphone initiative (see Collier & Whitehead 2023; Whitehead & Collier 2022).

Facebook first deployed its Voter Megaphone programme in 2008 and it has since been used in a number of national and local elections. The Voter Megaphone initiative is a quintessential digital nudge. It works on the premise of enabling people who have voted in an election to display an "I have voted" icon on their Facebook profile. Friends of those who have used the "I have voted" function can then see who among their friends has been to the polls. The Voter Megaphone thus combines the social influence of nudges (revealing who has voted), with the highly personalized prompts of digital nudges (when you see the names and faces of your own peers). The Voter Megaphone is also a prototypical hyper-nudge. The hyper-nudging element of the initiative is evident in both the scale of the nudge and its experimental quality. In one trial, for example, 61 million people were enrolled in a study to assess the impacts of the Voter Megaphone (Bond *et al.* 2012). This study discovered that the initiative increased voter turnout in one election by 340,000 people (from a population of 61 million). Facebook reassured users and regulators that the Voter Megaphone was non-partisan and simply sought to increase levels of engagement with the democratic process. However, concerns were understandably raised about the potential of such a tool to facilitate heightened voter turnout for certain political parties and voter suppression among others.

A final set of nudges are those that are being deployed to help to address the various social problems that are associated with the use of online platforms and digital devices. Although these nudges overlap with the operation of the choice editing and prompt-based nudges outlined above, their particular function is, we believe, worthy of a separate form of categorization. These nudges do not use digital platforms and smart technology to nudge people in socially and environmentally desirable directions. Instead, they focus on trying to address the problems associated with being on electronic devices in the first place. As has been well documented, the use of digital technology (and in particular social media platforms) is associated with a series of mental health and broader social problems. These problems are connected to: (1) the targeted feeding of messages to particular population segments which generate anxieties around, for example, social standing, body image and diet; and (2) the generally addictive nature of digital platforms and devices. Of course, the addictive nature of digital platforms is not an accident, as many Big Tech companies have deployed the insights of the behavioural and psychological sciences to try and maximize engagement with their systems (so we see the attention-grabbing signal of social approval that is the "Like" button and the failure to effectively regulate divisive and controversial digital content precisely because it grabs and holds people's attention) (Whitehead & Collier 2022). It is in these contexts that Big Tech companies have been utilizing nudges as a way of mitigating some of the worst effects of their products. It is interesting to note that some of the inspiration for the deployment of *nudges to prevent harm* comes from the gambling sector. Many Big Tech companies took their lead from the engagement tactics of gambling companies to try and generate addictive behaviours within their users (including targeted rewards and high levels of visual stimulation). The socio-economic problems generated by gambling (particularly in its online and digital forms) resulted in the sector (in certain countries) implementing nudges to mitigate their most harmful effects (see Jones *et al.* 2013). Related nudges sought to encourage gamblers to set spending limits before they started a gambling session (thus enabling Systems 2 thinking to set the limits of action before System 1 took over) or, in more extreme contexts, gamblers were prompted to sign up for voluntary self-exclusion schemes. Big Tech companies have followed the example set by the gambling sector and seek to deploy nudges to mitigate the worse effects of the psychological and behavioural power of their products.

A prominent recent example of Big Tech's deployment of nudges to prevent harm is provided by Meta's social networking service Instagram. Concerns have been raised over the impacts of Instagram on users' sense of self-worth and mental health, particularly teenage girls. Instagram's digital nudge targets teenagers who have spent a significant amount of time searching for potentially problematic topics (Forsey 2022). The nudge encourages users to reflect on the amount of time they are spending on the platform, while also suggesting other, more positive content. On these terms the nudge operates as a form of enforced pause which encourages users to engage with a more contemplative way of thinking about their use of social media. It is essentially a *nudge to think*. As with all nudges this attempt to try and prevent unhealthy outcomes from online experiences does not *stop* users from looking at content, but merely suggests alternative topics of interest. Interestingly, there appears to be a slightly more coercive element to this nudge, as it has been reported that, in addition to suggesting alternative content, the algorithmic nudge also deliberately hides potentially harmful material (see Forsey 2022). Instagram have also launched a "Take a Break" nudge, which is activated if teens have spent prolonged periods of time on the platform (*ibid.*). Caroline Forsey (2022) makes an interesting observation with regard to Instagram's nudge that excludes certain topics that may be associated with appearance comparison. In addition to potentially nudging teens away from harmful content, it could also act as a nudge for content developers who are using Instagram. If the algorithm nudges young people towards more positive content an immediate incentive is generated for the creation of more constructive content.

Critical perspectives on digital nudging

However well intentioned, it should come as little surprise that digital nudging in general, and hyper-nudging in particular, have been associated with a series of ethical and practical concerns (see Mills 2022; Whitehead & Collier 2022; Whitehead *et al.* 2018; Yeung 2016). Although digital nudging may ultimately use the same techniques as nudging in the analogue world, the systems of which many of them are a part make them distinctive (see Mills 2022). As Figure 5.4 demonstrates, each of the digital nudges we have described above is connected in one way or another with surveillance capitalism. As such digital nudging raises ethical questions which supersede those of older nudging regimes. Analogue nudging has long been subject to critiques that draw attention to their potential to undermine human autonomy, exploit behavioural frailties and deny our right to be wrong (see Jones *et al.* 2013; Furedi 2011b). But digital nudging, and hyper-nudging in particular, clearly raise the ethical stakes. These are nudges that are predicated on the erosion of privacy, and an ability to be able to prompt behavioural responses in private as well as public spheres. Perhaps most worrying of all is the idea that surveillance capitalist technologies can know us better than we know ourselves and exploit such knowledge for commercial gain. Ultimately, the immersive and bespoke nature of hyper-nudges makes their influence increasingly difficult to resist. As such, it raises important questions about the softness of the power that is associated with digital nudges, and whether any behavioural technology that is backed-up by surveillance capitalism can be really thought of as "easily avoidable".

The connection between digital nudging and surveillance capitalism raises further issues. If choice architectures are increasingly created and maintained within the corporate (Big Tech) sphere, and choice architects are non-human proprietorial algorithms, how can these systems be held to account? Furthermore, if hyper-nudging is being used by Big Tech, it is always likely that even personally and socially beneficial nudges are being mobilized primarily to yield behavioural data that will have commercial value. Perhaps this is a price worth paying, but it raises questions about the extent to which nudges enable us to do what we want, or get what we need, or whether they merely encourage us to behave in ways that others would ultimately like us to. The age of the hyper-nudge thus not only makes nudges harder to avoid, it also makes them more difficult to understand and politically contest.

Perhaps the most significant concern that is associated with hyper-nudges can be raised in relation to those nudges that seek to prevent digital harm. In essence, these nudges reflect surveillance capitalism mobilizing its own

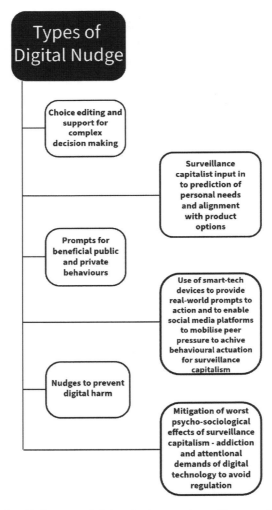

Figure 5.4 Relationship between digital nudge types and surveillance capitalism

techniques to solve the human problems that those same techniques have caused. But do we really believe that in an economic system which is driven by engagement and demand that surveillance capitalists can be trusted to regulate harmful levels of useage. Facebook's own engagement graph clearly demonstrates that the closer online content gets to controversial topics the higher the rates of engagement (Collier & Whitehead 2023). Can we really trust Big Tech's algorithms to constantly police the line between optimal levels of digital engagement for human wellbeing and the levels of engagement that will maximize surveillance capitalist revenues. In this complex system of people and technology and of nudge and counter-nudge, surely even the most sophisticated algorithm will inevitably fail in its quest to regulate itself. And herein lies the critical issue. In the age of digital nudging does the nudge embody an attempt by Big Tech to avoid meaningful regulation? In other words, could the hyper-nudge ultimately become the anti-regulatory device that some of its founders originally hoped it would be (see Chapter 2)?

Conclusion

In this chapter we have considered the emergence of nudging within digital life. We have revealed how digital nudging can take different forms, and while exhibiting the same techniques as analogue nudging, digital nudging is part of a very different operating system than its predecessors. This chapter has revealed that while digital nudging offers new opportunities for behavioural influence (particularly in terms of reach, personalization and learning) it also presents fresh ethical challenges. In particular we have argued that through its inescapable forms and connections with surveillance capitalism hyper-nudging is characterized by a far less gentle form of power than its analogue predecessors. In many ways digital nudging reflects the future of nudging that is already with us.

6

Conclusion

At the beginning of this book, we set out to address four questions: *what is nudging?; where has it come from?; should we use it?; and, where and when is it best applied?* By way of conclusion, we return to each of these questions.

What is nudging?

We have presented nudging as a distinctly gentle form of power. Nudging combines the insights of certain branches of the behavioural sciences into the irrational nature of human decision-making with insights from design science concerning the power of environmental stimuli. Put simply, nudging seeks neither to change the individual (through education or moral persuasion), or coerce people (through regulation or taxation), but rather to coax desired behaviours through a better understanding of our collective biases and decision-making environments. In summary, nudging:

1. Tends to target human unconscious bias as both a source of behavioural error and route to effective behavioural modification.
2. Is based upon a more-than-rational account of the human subject.
3. Offers alternative policy mechanisms to those traditionally associated with education, taxation and regulation.
4. Suggests new opportunities for intervention within areas of personal wellbeing.
5. Avoids coercive measures.

Throughout this volume, however, we have seen that nudging rarely exists in the world in its purest form. It more commonly exists in various hybrid forms and combinations. So, while nudging often operates at an unconscious level, targets human irrationality, and is distinct from educational policy, it can be used to raise awareness of an issue, prompt rational reflections, and support education (as is the case with emerging Nudge-plus approaches). We have also seen that despite being seemingly antithetical to coercion, in its digital (Nudge 2.0) forms nudging can be hard to avoid and resist.

Despite its association with gentle, suggestive forms of power, we have also seen that in generating new opportunities for states and corporations to legitimately intervene within our personal lives and wellbeing nudging challenges many of the shibboleths of liberal society, in particular the harm-to-others principle and the limits of legitimate state intervention. In these contexts, we recommend that when seeking to answer the question, "what is nudging?" it is best conceived of as a spectrum of psychological/ design-oriented approaches to a series of policy problems which can be traced back to the five core principles outlined above. Nudging, as it currently exists in the wild is, however, most commonly an adapted expression of these key features and is likely to be found in combination with other policy tools and approaches.

Where has nudging come from?

We have seen that nudging did not simply enter the world in 2008 with the publication of Thaler and Sunstein's highly influential book *Nudge*. Nudging has a long and complex prehistory, which encompasses the pioneering work of Herbert Simon, the experiments of social marketing, the emergence of cognitive design, and numerous practical policy developments aimed at changing people's behaviour. This prehistory overlaps with the rise of behavioural economics and the work of prominent thinkers such as Kahneman and Tversky, alongside Thaler and Sunstein, who are strongly associated with nudging. Acknowledging the diverse, and sometimes contradictory, history of nudging is, however, important because it reveals the heterodox perspectives that have informed the practice. These perspectives can often get overlooked within more recent attempts to package nudging as an anti-regulatory third way in policy. But the history of nudging introduced in this volume has shown uncertainty over the extent to which people can be empowered to overcome their own behavioural biases and what actually constitutes normality and rationality within human behaviour.

If nothing else, we hope that the history we've charted helps to reveal the *contingency of the present* in relation to nudging policies. What is described as nudging in the world today reflects a relatively narrow, and certainly politically constrained, interpretation of a much more diverse set of insights. Engaging more creatively with the history of ideas that have informed nudging enables us to question why it is that market compliant behaviours are seen as rational and why nudging appears to attribute the blame for market failures on individuals and not economic systems. If the science of nudging is based upon a realization that humans are not very effective market actors, one of its implications could be to question the increasing spread of market systems into various spheres of public life. Furthermore, if our fortunes are seen to be critically determined by the environments in which we live, why is greater emphasis not placed on improving the choice infrastructures of everyday life? At the heart of nudging there is the potential for a political project which challenges market orthodoxies and supports more significant forms of government investment in all aspects of public life. Nudging, in many of its current manifestations, is primarily anti-regulation in its orientation. But there are other lessons and alternative directions of travel that can be derived from the sciences of nudging. Of course, if these alterative perspectives are to be adopted, the term nudging may itself be anachronistic: denoting as it does a form of innocuous influence. But, it is important that any rejection of nudging does not result in the automatic rejection of is antecedent principles and perspectives.

Should we use nudging?

A significant thread throughout this book has been to question the ethics and efficacy of nudging. There are a series of reasons to doubt the efficacy of nudging. Many of the original trials on which nudges are based cannot be replicated; there have been incidents of data fraud; and there may be biases in the systems of scientific publication which have led to a significant overestimation of the likely impacts of nudging.

Despite nudging raising ethical concerns, ultimately it appears to be less ethically problematic than many people fear – at least in its analogue form.

So, while nudging may diminish the sense of moral responsibility we have for certain actions, and concomitantly reduce our ability learn from our mistakes, it does not remove our ability to develop moral sensibilities and responsibility in other areas of our lives where we are not being nudged.

The emergence of hyper-nudging and Nudge 2.0 systems does raise new questions in terms of efficacy and ethics. It appears that hyper-nudging may be more effective in promoting behaviour change at large scales and over longer periods of time. However, the fact that hyper-nudging is often part of surveillance capitalist systems means that Nudge 2.0 presents more significant ethical problems. A key insight of this book has been to emphasize that questions concerning the ethics and efficacy of nudging need to be considered together. The ethics and efficacy of nudging exist on a spectrum with some nudges being more effective than others, while some may raise more ethical challenges then others. It is important therefore to continually ask whether the effects of nudging justify the ethical challenges of eroded moral independence and political accountability they may raise. The more effective a policy is the more willing we may be to tolerate its ethical downsides. The systems within which nudges operated (democratically accountable government versus proprietorial Big Tech companies) are also likely to be a key consideration when calibrating efficacy gains and ethical loses.

Where and when is nudging best applied?

In many ways, we have challenged the premise of this question. To answer effectively, we first need to ask what type of nudge is being applied and in which circumstance. In general terms, we have seen that nudging tends to be most effective when being used to address relatively simple behaviours or single-choice actions. For example, it is claimed that some of the most successful applications of nudging have been evident in attempts to get people to sign-up to pension schemes and join organ donor registers. But, it is within nudging's heartlands of success that we can also discern its limitations. So, even though a nudge can encourage more people to join organ donor registers, this does not address the difficult decisions that family members have to make following the death of a loved one. Similarly, getting people to join a pension scheme does not necessarily solve the problem of pension poverty if economic circumstances mean that people have to take out loans against their pensions simply to make ends meet in the here and now.

In these contexts, we claim that at its best nudging can be used to support more effective human decision-making in potentially empowering ways. For this to happen, however, it is important that nudges are part of systems that have transparency and accountability built into them. It is also important that nudges are not just seen as a cheap and easy alternatives to more substantial changes in the structures that shape human opportunity and wellbeing. The key insight here is not so much related to when and when not to use nudges, but about not seeing nudges as policy ends in themselves. We would thus encourage heterodox experiments with the varied insights associated with nudging in order to extend what it may be possible for public policy to achieve and, if nothing else, to focus minds on the complexities of human motivation and behaviour. But we would encourage nudging to be seen primarily as a tool that is at its best when deployed to support wider forms of regulation and infrastructural investment. It is in combination with other forms of intervention that nudging is best placed to support a deep and lasting commitment to improving collective health, wealth and happiness.

References

Akelof, G. & R. Schiller 2010. *Animal Spirits: How Human Psychology Drives the Economy, and Why It Matters for Global Capitalism*. Princeton, NJ: Princeton University Press.

Allemandi, L. *et al.* 2015. "Sodium content in processed foods in Argentina: compliance with the national law". *Cardiovascular Diagnosis and Therapy* 5: 197–206. https://doi.org/10.3978/j.issn.2223-3652.2015.04.01.

Altmann, S., A. Grunewald & J. Radbruch 2022. "Interventions and cognitive spillovers." *Reviews of Economic Studies* 89: 2293–328. https://doi.org/10.1093/restud/rdab087.

Ariely, D. 2009. *Predictably Irrational: The Hidden Forces That Shape Our Decisions*. New York: HarperCollins.

Banerjee, S. & P. John 2021. "Nudge plus: incorporating reflection into behavioural public policy". *Behavioural Public Policy* April: 1–16. https://doi.org/10.1017/bpp.2021.6.

BBC 2016. "Health professionals call for alcohol-only check outs". BBC News, 11 February. https://www.bbc.co.uk/news/uk-scotland-35548784.

Binkley, S. 2009. "The work of neoliberal governmentality: temporality and ethical substance in the tale of two dads". *Foucault Studies* 6: 60–78. https://doi.org/10.22439/fs.v0i0.2472.

Bond, R. *et al.* 2012. "A 61-million-person experiment in social influence and political mobilization". *Nature* 489: 295–8. https://doi.org/10.1038/nature11421.

Bradon, E. 2022. "Realistic reasons to be bullish about nudging". *Behavioural Scientist*, 26 September. https://behavioralscientist.org/realistic-reasons-to-be-bullish-on-nudging/.

Briscese, G. & C. Tan 2018. *Applying Behavioural Insights to Labour Markets*. Behavioural Insights Team. https://www.bi.team/wp-content/uploads/2018/11/TheBehavioural InsightsTeam-LabourMarketsReport.pdf.

Button, M. 2018. "Bounded rationality without bounded democracy: nudges, democratic citizenship, and pathways for building civic capacity." *Perspectives on Politics* 16: 1034–52. https://doi.org/10.1017/S1537592718002086

Camerer, C. *et al.* 2003. "Regulation for conservatives: behavioral economics and the case for 'asymmetric paternalism'". *University of Pennsylvania Law Review* 151: 1211–54. https://doi.org/10.2307/3312889.

Carlsson, F. *et al.* 2021. "The use of green nudges as an environmental policy instrument". *Review of Environmental Economics and Policy* 15: 216–37. https://doi.org/10.1086/715524.

Carnegie, D. 1936. *How to Win Friends and Influence People*. London: Vermillion.

Carter, E. 2015. "Making the Blue Zones: neoliberalism and nudges in public health promotion". *Social Science and Medicine* 133: 374–82. https://doi.org/10.1016/j.socscimed.2015.

01.019.Chater, N. & G. Lowenstein 2022. "The i-frame and the s-frame: how focusing on individual-level solutions has led behavioral public policy astray". *Behavioural and Brain Sciences* Sep 5: 1–60. https://doi.org/10.1017/S0140525X22002023.

Chatziathanasiou, K. 2022. "Nudging after the replication crisis: on uncertain effects of behavioral governance and the way forward". Verfassungsblog, 30 August. https://verfassungsblog.de/nudging-after-the-replication-crisis/.

Chriss, J. 2015. "Nudging and social marketing". *Society* 52: 54–61.

Cole, D. 2014. "*Nudger in Chief*: how, and why, Cass Sunstein believes laws and public policies should help save us from our irrational impulses". *The Atlantic*, May. https://www.theatlantic.com/magazine/archive/2014/05/our-nudge-in-chief/359804/.

Collier, W. & M. Whitehead 2023. "Corporate governmentality: building the empirical and theoretical case". *Territory, Politics, Governance* 11: 1029–48. https://doi.org/10.1080/21622671.2022.2153159.

Conly, S. 2012. *Against Autonomy: Justifying Coercive Paternalism*. Cambridge: Cambridge University Press.

Cowley, J. 2017. "A hesitant radical in an age of Trump: David Brooks and search for moderation". *New Statesman*, 26 October. https://www.newstatesman.com/encounter/2017/10/hesitant-radical-age-trump-david-brooks-and-search-moderation.

Crompton, T. 2010. *Common Cause: The Case for Working with our Cultural Values*. https://assets.wwf.org.uk/downloads/common_cause_report.pdf.

DEFRA 2007. *A Framework for Pro-Environmental Behaviours*. London: Department for Food, Environment and Rural Affairs.

DellaVigna, S. & E. Linos 2022. "RCTs to scale: comprehensive evidence from two nudge units". *Econometrica* 90: 81–116. https://doi.org/10.3982/ECTA18709.

Feitsma, J. & M. Whitehead 2022. "Bounded interdisciplinarity: critical interdisciplinary perspectives on context and evidence in behavioural public policies". *Behavioural Public Policy* 6: 358–84. https://doi.org/10.1017/bpp.2019.30.

Fogg, B. 1998. "Persuasive computers: perspectives and research directions". Proceeding of the SIGGHI Conference on Human Factors in Computing Systems, 225–32. https://doi.org/10.1145/274644.274677.

Forsey, C. 2022. "How Instagram's new nudge feature for teens could impact marketers or creators". Hubspot 22 June. https://blog.hubspot.com/marketing/instagram-nudge-feature.

Furedi, F. 2011a. *On Tolerance: A Defence of Moral Independence*. London: Continuum.

Furedi, F. 2011b. "Defending moral autonomy against an army of nudgers". Spiked. https://www.spiked-online.com/2011/01/20/defending-moral-autonomy-against-an-army-of-nudgers/.

Gigerenzer, G. 2015. *Risk Savvy: How to Make God Decisions*. London: Penguin.

Goswami, I. & O. Urminsky 2016. "When should the ask be a nudge? The effect of default amounts on charitable donations". *Journal of Marketing Research* 53: 829–46.

Hall, J. & J. Madsen 2022. "Can behavioral interventions be too salient? Evidence from traffic safety messages". *Science* 376(6591). https://doi.org/10.1126/science.abm3427.

Hallsworth, M. 2023. *A Manifesto for Applying Behavioural Science*. Behavioural Insights Team. https://www.bi.team/wp-content/uploads/2023/04/BIT_Manifesto.pdf.

Hallsworth, M. & E. Kirkman 2020. *Behavioural Insights*. Cambridge, MA: MIT Press.

Halpern, D. 2016. *Inside the Nudge Unit: How Small Changes Can Make a Big Difference*. London: W. H. Allen.

Halpern, D. & M. Sanders 2016. "Nudging by government: progress, impact, and lessons learned". *Behavioural Science and Policy* 2: 53–65. https://behavioralpolicy.org/wp-content/uploads/2017/06/Sanders-web.pdf.

Head, B. 2022. *Wicked Problems in Public Policy: Understanding and Responding to Complex Challenges*. London: Palgrave Macmillan.

Hirsch, P. 2021. "Beyond the first nudge: the case for behavioural science in corporate practice". Ogilvy, 6 February. https://www.ogilvy.com/ideas/beyond-first-nudge-case-behavioral-science-corporate-practice.

House of Lords (Science and Technology Committee) 2011. *Behaviour Change*. Second Report. https://publications.parliament.uk/pa/ld201012/ldselect/ldsctech/179/17902.htm.

Howell, R. 2011. "Lights, camera … action? Altered attitudes and behaviour in response to the climate change film *The Age of Stupid*". *Global Environmental Change* 21: 177–87. http://dx.doi.org/10.1016/j.gloenvcha.2010.09.004.

IFPRI 2016. *Global Nutrition Report 2016. From Promise to Impact: Ending Malnutrition by 2030*. Washington, DC: International Food Policy Research Institute. https://globalnutritionreport.org/reports/2016-global-nutrition-report/#:~:text=From%20promise%20to%20impact%3A%20Ending,ways%20to%20reverse%20this%20trend.

IJzerman, H. *et al.* 2020. "Use caution when applying behavioural science to policy". *Nature Human Behaviour* 4: 1092–94. https://doi.org/10.1038/s41562-020-00990-w.

Isin, E. 2004. "The neurotic citizen". *Citizenship Studies* 8: 217–35.

Jesse, M. & D. Jannach 2021. "Digital nudging with recommender systems: survey and future directions". *Computers in Human Behaviour Reports* 3. https://doi.org/10.1016/j.chbr.2020.100052.

John, P. *et al.* 2011. *Nudge, Nudge, Think, Think: Experimenting with Ways to Change Civic Behaviour*. London: Bloomsbury.

Johnson, D. 2016. "Twilight of the nudges: the quest to keep behavioral economics in policy after Obama's presidency". *The New Republic*, 27 October. https://newrepublic.com/article/138175/twilight-nudges.

Jones, R. & M. Whitehead 2018. "'Politics done like science': critical perspectives on psychological governance and the experimental state". *Environment and Planning D: Society and Space* 36: 313–30. https://doi.org/10.1177/0263775817748330.

Jones, R., J. Pykett & M. Whitehead 2013a. *Changing Behaviours: On the Rise of the Psychological State*. Cheltenham: Elgar.

Jones, R., J. Pykett & M. Whitehead 2013b. "Behaviour change policies in the UK: an anthropological perspective". *Geoforum* 48: 33–41. https://doi.org/10.1016/j.geoforum.2013.03.012.

Kahneman, D. 2011. *Thinking, Fast and Slow*. London: Penguin.

Kahneman, D. & G. Klein 2009. "Conditions for intuitive expertise: a failure to disagree". *American Psychologist* 64: 515–26. https://doi.org/10.1037/a0016755.

Kahneman, D. & A. Tversky 1974. "Judgment under uncertainty: heuristics and biases". *Science* 185: 1124–31. https://doi.org/10.1126/science.185.4157.1124.

Kahneman, D. & A. Tversky 1979. "Prospect theory: an analysis of decision under risk". *Econometrica* 47: 263–91. https://doi.org/10.2307/1914185.

Kristal, A. *et al.* 2020. "When we're wrong, it's our responsibility as scientists to say so". *Scientific American*, 21 March. https://blogs.scientificamerican.com/observations/when-were-wrong-its-our-responsibility-as-scientists-to-say-so/.

Leggett, W. 2014. "The politics of behaviour change: nudge, neoliberalism, and the state". *Policy and Politics* 42: 3–19. https://doi.org/10.1332/030557312X655576.

Lewis, M. 2017. *The Undoing Project: A Friendship that Changed the World*. London: Penguin.

Lin, Y., M. Osman & R. Ashcroft 2017. "Nudge: concept, effectiveness, ethics". *Basic and Applied Social Psychology* 30: 293–306. https://doi.org/10.1080/01973533.2017.1356304.

Lindbeck, A. (ed.) 1992. *Nobel Lectures, Economics 1969–1980*. Singapore: World Scientific.

Lockton, D. 2012. "Simon's scissors and ecological psychology in design for behaviour change". SSRN, 6 August. http://dx.doi.org/10.2139/ssrn.2125405.

Lowenstein, G. & N. Chater 2017. "Putting nudges in perspective". *Behavioural Public Policy* 1: 26–53. https://doi.org/10.1017/bpp.2016.7.

Lowenstein, G., T. Brennan & K. Volpp 2007. "Asymmetric paternalism to improve health behaviours". *Journal of the America Medical Association* 289: 2415–17. https://doi.org/10.1001/jama.298.20.2415.

Luo, Y. *et al.* 2022. "A meta-analytic cognitive framework of nudge and sludge". Preprint. https://doi.org/10.21203/rs.3.rs-2089594/v1

Mill, J. 1859. *On Liberty*. London: Penguin.

Mills, S. 2022. "Finding the nudge in hypernudge". *Technology and Society* 71. https://doi.org/10.1016/j.techsoc.2022.102117.

Morgan, S. & J. Miller 2002. "Communicating about gifts of life: the effect of knowledge, attitudes, and altruism on behavior and behavioral intentions regarding organ donation". *Journal of Applied Communication Research* 30: 163–78. http://dx.doi.org/10.1080/00909880216580.

Norman, D. 1981. "The truth about Unix: the user interface is horrid". *Datamation* 27(12). http://www.ceri.memphis.edu/people/smalley/ESCI7205_misc_files/The_truth_about_Unix_cleaned.pdf.

Norman, D. 2013. *The Design of Everyday Things*. Cambridge, MA: MIT Press.

OECD 2017. *Behavioural Insights and Public Policy: Lessons from Around the World*. https://www.oecd.org/gov/regulatory-policy/behavioural-insights-and-public-policy-9789264270480-en.htm.

Oliver, A. 2017. *The Origins of Behavioural Public Policy*. Cambridge: Cambridge University Press.

Open Science Collaboration 2015. "Estimating the reproducibility of psychological science". *Science* 349. https://doi.org/10.1126/science.aac4716.

Packard, V. 2007. *The Hidden Persuaders*. New York: Ig Publishing.

Petticrew, M. *et al.* 2020. "Dark nudges and sludge in big alcohol: behavioral economics, cognitive biases, and alcohol industry corporate social responsibility". *Millbank Quarterly*, December: 1290–328. https://doi.org/10.1111/1468-0009.12475.

Pykett, J., R. Jones & M. Whitehead (eds) 2016. *Psychological Governance and Public Policy: Governing the Mind, Brain and Behaviour*. Abingdon: Routledge.

Risdon, C. 2017. "Scaling nudges with machine learning". *Behavioral Scientist*, 25 October. www.behavioralscientist.org/scaling-nudges-machine-learning/.

Rose, N. 1998. *Inventing Ourselves: Psychology, Power, and Personhood*. Cambridge: Cambridge University Press.

Rose, N. 2010. "'Screen and intervene': governing risky brains". *History of the Human Sciences* 23: 79–105.

Runciman, D. 2021. *Confronting Leviathan: A History of Ideas*. London: Profile.

Schatzki, T. 2002. *The Site of Social: A Philosophical Account of the Constitution of Social Life and Change*. University Park, PA: Pennsylvania State University Press.

Schneider, C., M. Weinmann & J. vom Brocke 2018. "Digital nudging: guiding online user choices through interface design". *Communications of the ACM* 61: 67–73.

Shu, L. *et al.* 2012. "Signing at the beginning makes ethics salient and decreases dishonest self-reports in comparison to signing at the end". *Psychological and Cognitive Sciences* 109: 15197–200. https://doi.org/10.1073/pnas.2115397118.

Simon, H. 1997. *Administrative Behaviour*. Fourth edn. New York: Free Press.

Simonsen, K. 1991. "Towards an understanding of the contextuality of modern life". *Environment and Planning D: Society and Space* 9: 417–31. https://doi.org/10.1068/d090417.

Smith, J. 2022. *The Internet Is Not What You Think It Is: A History, A Philosophy, A Warning*. Princeton, NJ: Princeton University Press.

Sunstein, C. 2013. *Simpler: The Future of Government*. New York: Simon & Schuster.

Sunstein, C. 2019. *On Freedom*. Princeton, NJ: Princeton University Press.

Sunstein, C., L. Reisch & J. Rauber 2017. "A worldwide consensus on nudging? Not quite, but almost". *Regulation and Governance* 12: 3–22. https://doi.org/10.1111/rego.12161.

Thaler, R. 2016. *Misbehaving: The Making of Behavioural Economics*. London: Penguin.

Thaler, R. 2017. Nobel Prize in Economic Sciences 2017, banquet speech. YouTube. https://www.youtube.com/watch?v=s6cruZhEB0o.

Thaler, R. & C. Sunstein 2003. "Libertarian paternalism". *American Economic Review* 93: 175–9. https://doi.org/10.1257/000282803321947001.

Thaler, R. & C. Sunstein 2008. *Nudge: Improving Decisions About Health Wealth and Happiness*. London: Penguin.

Thaler, R. & C. Sunstein 2022. *Nudge: The Final Edition*. London: Allen Lane.

UNAIDS 2000. *Condom Social Marketing: Selected Case Studies*. Geneva: UNAIDS.

Walker, S. 2004. *Three Mile Island: A Nuclear Crisis in Historical Perspective*. Berkeley, CA: University of California Press.

Weinmann, M., C. Schneider & J. vom Brocke 2016. "Digital nudging". *Business & Information Systems Engineering* 58: 433–6. https://doi.org/10.1007/s12599-016-0453-1.

Welsh, M. *et al.* 2016. "The 'problem gambler' and socio-spatial vulnerability". In F. Gobet & M. Schiller (eds), *Problem Gambling: Cognition, Prevention and Treatment*, 156–87. London: Palgrave Macmillan.

White, M. 2013. *The Manipulation of Choice: Ethics and Libertarian Paternalism*. London: Palgrave Macmillan.

Whitehead, M. 2019. "Nudging around the world: a critical geography of the behaviour change agenda". In H. Strassheim & S. Beck (eds), *Handbook of Behavioural Change and Public Policy*, 90–101. Cheltenham: Elgar.

Whitehead, M. 2020. "Shoshana Zuboff, *The Age of Surveillance Capitalism: The Fight for a Human Future at the New Frontier of Power*: a review essay". *Antipode Intervention*. https://antipodeonline.org/wp-content/uploads/2019/10/Book-review_Whitehead-on-Zuboff.pdf.

Whitehead, M. & W. Collier 2022. *Smart-Tech Society: Convenience, Control and Resistance*. Cheltenham: Elgar.

Whitehead, M., R. Jones & J. Pykett 2020. "Questioning post-political perspectives on the psychological state: behavioural public policy in the Netherlands". *Environment and Planning C: Politics and Space* 38: 214–32. https://doi.org/10.1177/2399654419867711.

Whitehead, M. *et al.* 2014. *Nudging all Over the World.* ESRC Report. https://changing behaviours.files.wordpress.com/2014/09/nudgedesignfinal.pdf.

Whitehead, M. *et al.* 2018. *Neuroliberalism: Behavioural Government in the Twenty-First Century.* Abingdon: Routledge.

Yeung, K. 2016. "'Hypernudge': big data as a mode of regulation by design". *Information, Communication and Society* 20: 118–36. https://doi.org/10.1080/1369118X.2016.1186713.

Zaltzman, J. 2018. "Ten years of Israel's organ transplant law: is it on the right track?". *Israel Journal of Health Policy Research* 7: 1–3. https://doi.org/10.1186/s13584-018-0232-1.

Zuboff, S. 2015. "Big other: surveillance capitalism and the prospects of an information civilization". *Journal of Information Technology* 30: 75–89. https://doi.org/10.1057/jit.2015.

Zuboff, S. 2016. "The secrets of surveillance capitalism". *Frankfurter Allegemeine*, 5 March. https://www.faz.net/aktuell/feuilleton/debatten/the-digital-debate/shoshana-zuboff-secrets-of-surveillance-capitalism-14103616.html.

Zuboff, S. 2019. *The Age of Surveillance Capitalism: The Fight for a Human Future at the New Frontier of Power.* London: Profile.

Index

libertarianism 13, 41
liberty 12 *see also* freedom
  personal 37, 39, 65
loss aversion 25, 29, 31, 89, 90, 93

manipulation 15, 52, 62, 78–9, 80, 95
markets 3
  financial 40
marketing 28–32, 54, 99
  industry 28
  social 29, 30, 108
  techniques 28–9
mechanistic thinking 66, 69
mini-budget (UK) 9
mistakes 25, 54, 110 *see also* human
  error
mobile phones 11

nanny state 12
neoliberalism 3, 47, 56, 62
Nobel Prize in Economics 19, 20, 21, 28
norms 71
  compliance 5
  constitutional 16
  libertarian 16
  social 5, 9, 14, 30, 48, 53, 54, 59, 62, 70,
    78, 93
nudge
  and Think 81
  critiques of 15, 49, 65, 66, 69, 73, 80,
    81, 82, 83, 103
  dark 41
  efficacy of 16, 69, 83, 109, 110
  globalization of 4, 43
  green 61–2
  honesty 68, 69
  hybrid 6, 108
  hyper- 86, 91–7, 99–100, 103–05, 110
  plus 81, 108
  power of 6, 13
  success 74, 110
  theorists 11
  Unit 4, 31, 41, 67
nudgestock 31
Nudge-think 11 *see also* Nudge and Think

nudging
  as a movement 37
  digital 17, 85, 86–105, 108
  ethical applications 32
  future of 85–105
  history of 19–43, 108–09
  holistic 70
  libertarian 35, 36–41
  limitations of 22, 72, 110
  non-western origins of 30–31
  popularity 4, 19, 46, 85

Obama, Barack 4, 42
obesity 12, 16, 39, 47, 50
Office of Information and Regulatory
  Affairs 4, 42, 65
opt-out systems 13, 74, 75
organ donation 57–8, 75–6
  in Israel 4, 58–9
organ donor register 5, 8, 13, 75–6, 79,
  110

paternalism 12, 39, 41, 79
  asymmetric 37–8
  coercive 37
  democratic 37
  libertarian 36, 37, 38
  soft 12, 36
pathology 28
  behavioural 2, 40
peer pressure 41, 70, 89
pensions (also pension savings) 5, 8, 10,
  13, 54, 73–5, 76, 97, 100, 110
persuasion 1, 2, 30
  moral 61, 107
  social 29
portion size 5–7 *see also* soda ban
power 1, 8, 16, 85, 96, 97, 100, 108
  of algorithms 96, 100
  gentle 2, 12, 16, 41, 95, 107
  of norms 30
  psychological 3, 15, 102
  soft 6, 13, 78, 103
  surveillance 105
presumed consent 57–8, 75–6